For our dear Susan
from
Papa & Mama

Manila - November 21, 1962

15.75
———
NHH

Also By Jean Slaughter

HORSEMANSHIP FOR BEGINNERS:
Riding, Jumping, and Schooling

with photographs by
MICHAEL J. PHILLIPS

A Borzoi Book for Young People
Published by Alfred A. Knopf

Pony Care

Alfred A. Knopf : New York

Pony Care

JEAN SLAUGHTER

photographs by HUGH ROGERS

To Christopher

L. C. Catalog card number 61–6054

THIS IS A BORZOI BOOK,
PUBLISHED BY ALFRED A. KNOPF, INC.

Copyright © 1961 by Jean Slaughter
All rights reserved. No part of this book may be reproduced in any form without permission in writing from the publisher, except by a reviewer who may quote brief passages and reproduce not more than three illustrations in a review to be printed in a magazine or newspaper. Manufactured in the United States of America. Published simultaneously in Canada by McClelland & Stewart, Ltd.

Acknowledgment

I would like to express my gratitude and thanks to those who helped, in so many ways, in the preparation of this book.

—To John H. Nickerson, D. V. M., for reading and checking the manuscript of this book.

—To Miss Felicia Townsend and to Mr. Otto H. Heuckeroth for their interest and advice in the discussions we held while this book was written.

—To J. D. Weiss, D. V. M., for checking the final manuscript; and to Robert Cornell, Jr., D. V. M. and C. E. Guthrie, D. V. M., for their kindness and patience in answering countless questions.

—To the Board of Stewards and members of the Ox Ridge Hunt Club in Darien, Conn., for lending their ponies and the use of their grounds for many of the photographs.

—To the young riders who spent so many uncomplaining and hard-working hours with their ponies while the photographs were taken: Jennifer Bates; Nancy Colhoun; Whitney Davis; Ann Kellam; Whitney Ann, Edwin, and Peter Neville; Caroline Sherman; Mary White; and David Wright.

—To Mr. Gerald J. Varden and Mr. Patrick J. McCollough, for their help with the countless details of preparation of ponies and equipment for the photographs.

—To Mrs. A. E. Luders, Jr., Mrs. Lyn Westerlund Taylor, Mrs. Nancy Moran Vidmer, and Master Peter Rose, for permission to use their photographs; to Mrs. James I. Raymond for the use of her Hackney Pony, *Banners Bright;* and to Mr. and Mrs. Robert W. Martin, Mr. and Mrs. F. J. Metzger, and Mr. and Mrs. James G. Rogers, Jr., for their kind permission to use their grounds for many of the photographs.

Photographs on pages 15, 19, 30, 35, 50, 66, 68, 80, and 88 by the author; all others by Hugh Rogers.

Contents

1. A PONY OF YOUR OWN — 3
2. HANDLING — 17
3. STABLING AND PADDOCKS — 31
4. CARE OF THE STALL — 41
5. FEEDING AND WATERING — 45
6. GROOMING — 57
7. COLD AND HOT WEATHER CARE — 67
8. YOUR PONY'S HOOFS AND LEGS — 77
9. ILLNESS AND FIRST AID — 88
10. SELECTION AND CARE OF TACK — 103
11. YOU AND YOUR PONY — 107

Glossary — 109
Points of the Pony — 111
Index — *follows page* 111

Pony Care

A Pony of Your Own

A pony of your own—what magic words! But whether you have had a someday-promise of a pony, or are ready to start your pony hunting at once, there are a number of things to consider before you begin.

Hardest of all, but most important of all, do not let your impatience run away with your common sense. Be sure you are ready for a pony of your own. Do you have a comfortable and convenient place to keep him, ready for him the moment he arrives? Do you know how to ride? (You certainly need not be an expert rider before you can have your own pony, but you should at least have had enough instruction to feel comfortable and secure on a pony's back.) Can you put a halter on a pony, and lead him, and handle him with confidence? And, once the first excitement has worn off, are you sure you are prepared to care for him with daily chores in wind and rain and snow and cold, no matter what else you would rather be doing at that moment?

Riding and handling knowledge can be gained through experience, whether you take a number of lessons at a riding stable, or practice with a friend's pony. But the question of daily care is not as easily answered. This is up to you.

A pony is not a bicycle which can be tucked into a corner of the garage and forgotten until the next time you want to ride. But you are probably well aware of this, and still prepared and willing to accept the responsibilities of a pony's daily care. And though it is important to consider the drawbacks, the chances are you will find yourself enjoying the challenge of caring for a pony of your own.

FINDING YOUR PONY

First of all, do not buy any pony sight unseen! Even if the pony is offered as a gift, see him and try him first, before you make up

THERE ARE PONIES OF MANY BREEDS, TYPES, AND SIZES

your mind. It is easy to acquire a pony. It is not a simple matter to get rid of him if he is unsuitable.

Watch for newspaper advertisements; call on the riding stables in your neighborhood; go to pony and horse shows and do not hesitate to speak to the owners of ponies you like. Their ponies might be for sale, or they might have others at home. It may take some time before you find a pony you like at the price you want to pay, but it is important for you not to become discouraged, or settle for just any pony that comes along. It is hard to be patient when you want a pony so badly, but when you find the right one, you will be well rewarded for waiting.

HOW MUCH SHOULD YOU PAY?

The price of a pony depends on so many things, some of which are his age, his breeding, and the amount of breaking, training, and schooling he has been given. You might find an unbroken pony colt for as little as fifty dollars (though this would be a very poor investment). On the other hand, if you wanted a highly bred, finely schooled show pony, you would probably find he would cost thou-

sands of dollars. Pony prices vary from one part of this country to another, but for a nice pony to keep at home just for fun, you should be able to find one for between one and two hundred dollars. If you want a special breed of pony, or one who is a good jumper, or a pony to hunt or to show, then you must be prepared to pay more for him.

Beware of the bargain pony, such as the one who is in such poor condition, so thin and miserable, that his owner says he will let you have him at a ridiculous price "just so he gets a good home." If you take a pony like this and feed him well, ninety-nine times out of a hundred you will soon find yourself the owner of a pony so full of meanness or bad habits that he had to be starved into being quiet enough to be sold. A few weeks of good care and proper feeding will bring all the old tricks back and you will be left with an impossible and worthless pony on your hands.

Another bargain approach is the word "if." "*If* he didn't have that bit of a bump on his knee, he would be worth thousands," or "*If* this pony had a fine rider like you to handle him, he would go like a lamb."

The "if" in these ponies is a word of warning. Do not buy other people's mistakes. They can bring you nothing but disappointment.

A PONY OF SHETLAND TYPE

WHAT TO LOOK FOR

No matter what kind of pony you are looking for, *manners* and *suitability* are the first requirements. But these qualities in a pony do *not* mean that he must be slow and dull to ride. Quite the contrary. A pony with manners—a pony suitable as a mount for a young rider—must be willing and cheerfully obedient, fun to ride, but responsive to control, quiet and easily handled in the stable—a pony whose general temperament combines alertness with kindness and common sense.

A WELL-MANNERED PUREBRED SHETLAND PONY

THE SAME PONY COMBINES MANNERS WITH ABILITY—A GOOD MOUNT FOR A YOUNG RIDER

This sounds like a lot to ask and to look for, but without manners and suitability, the most handsome of ponies is worthless. Unless the pony you are considering has these essential qualities, you should forget him and look for another.

Conformation (a pony's general appearance and build) matters, not because outward handsomeness is all-important, but because a pony with good conformation is what a horseman would call "well put together." It would be just about impossible to find any pony with absolutely perfect conformation. But a pony can have several minor conformation faults and still give the over-all appearance a good pony should have—a look of symmetry and of balanced proportion, no matter what his breed or type.

A STURDY, DEPENDABLE, LARGE PONY OF UNKNOWN BREEDING

(If you are not familiar with the terms used in describing the points of a pony in the following paragraphs, you will find them in the diagram on page 111.)

The head should have a finely shaped muzzle, eyes that are large and set well apart (width between the eyes is considered to be a sign of intelligence) and ears that are carried in an alert, interested manner. The expression of a good head gives an over-all impression of intelligence, interest, and common sense.

The neck should join the head in a clean line at the throat, and it should arch slightly from the ears to the *withers* (the highest point at the top of a pony's shoulder).

Avoid the pony with a thick, stubby neck and heavy shoulders. He will be a poor mover.

The shoulders should show a definite slope in angle from the withers to the point of the shoulder and they should be clean lined and well defined. A good shoulder is important, because a pony must have good shoulders to move well.

(If you have any doubt, look at the pony while he is wearing

THIS LOVELY LITTLE PONY IS BY A WELSH STALLION OUT OF A SHETLAND MARE

a saddle. A lot of shoulder will show in front of the saddle on a good pony. On a pony with poor shoulders, the saddle will look almost as though it is sitting right up on his neck.)

Look for a short back and ribs well sprung. This means ribs which arch out nicely behind the saddle. A flat-sided pony (who usually has a narrow chest, as well) is called *weedy*. Weedy ponies always look scrawny, no matter how well they are fed, and they lack strength and endurance.

Too round a *barrel* is a fault often found in ponies of the Shetland type which have big, heavy heads, thick, short necks, and straight shoulders. Some of these ponies may look sweet, but they move with a hard, short stride and they are not usually much fun to ride.

The *rump* should be square and strong. It should not run down at an angle to the top of the tail; an angled rump is called a "goose rump" and is accompanied by weak hindquarters and legs.

The hind legs should be sturdy and well muscled right down to the *hock*. When seen from behind, they should be parallel to each other; hocks that point in toward each other are called "cow hocks," and they are a weakness. After all, the hindquarters and hind legs are the driving power of a pony, and it is important that they be strong and well made.

The chest should be square and of good breadth, with the forelegs set well apart and strongly muscled down to the knee. The knee itself should be well defined, broad and flat, and the leg tendons should be straight and clean in line.

The *fetlock joints* on all four legs should be free from puffiness or swelling; the *pasterns* should slope slightly, down to neat and well-shaped hoofs. (The forehoofs are always rounder than the hind hoofs.)

All in all, look for a pony who stands and moves with a natural balance and who carries himself well—a pony who, in over-all appearance, gives you the impression of strength without coarseness and fineness of line without weakness.

Basic requirements for good conformation do not vary whether

A PUREBRED HACKNEY PONY UNDER SADDLE

A PUREBRED HACKNEY PONY IN HARNESS

you are looking for a crossbred pony to ride just for fun, or a finely bred pony to hunt or show. But different types and breeds do have subtle conformation differences. It is always a good idea to have an experienced horseman with you when you go to look at a pony. If you are trying to find an especially fine pony of a particular breed, it is *essential* that you take someone with you who is a qualified expert in that breed.

TRYING THE PONY

When you have had a good look at your pony prospect and if you like his type, size, and general conformation, ask to have him put back in the stall. Put the pony's halter on by yourself. Turn him around in the stall, pick up his feet, and handle him thoroughly, while you watch for signs of resentment or disobedience.

Lead him out of the stall yourself. Saddle and bridle him and lead him out of the stable. Do not let anyone hold him or help you while you mount, fix your stirrups, and straighten your reins. If the pony must be held while these things are done, what will you do if you have to dismount and get on again out on a ride by yourself? Above anything else, you certainly do not want a pony you cannot handle alone.

Ride the pony at a walk until you and he know each other, then at a trot and canter. Ride him in a ring if you want to, at first, but if you like the pony and are seriously interested in him, be sure to try him outside the ring as well, and out on the roads if possible.

Take a friend who can ride with you, if you can, and ask him to ride and handle the pony while you watch. Through all of this, look for obedience, willingness, and a cheerful disposition. At the very least, the pony should go along on an easy rein, walking, trotting, and cantering without fussing or having to be pushed along at every stride. And, no matter what kind of a pony you are looking for, ask yourself these questions about him: Can he do the job you

THIS PONY IS BY AN ARABIAN OUT OF A THOROUGHBRED MARE

A TRUSTWORTHY, KIND-TEMPERED PONY CAN BE FUN FOR THE WHOLE FAMILY

want him to do? Has he the ability to do it well?

When you have found a pony you like, ask the owner if you may have it checked (or "vetted") by a veterinarian of your choice. If the owner refuses, you may be sure there is something the matter with the pony, and you should promptly forget him. Any good horseman knows that the buying and selling of ponies is an uncertain business at best. For the owner's protection as well as yours, the pony should be examined by a veterinarian before you take him home.

The vet will check the pony's eyesight, breathing, and heart; he will examine him for soundness and for any serious blemish that might one day cause lameness. If the pony passes the vetting with flying colors, you will have the assurance that you are starting your new ownership well, and this is worth far more to you than the vet's small fee. (Imagine how you would feel if the pony you bought turned out to be incurably lame, for instance, or had a bad heart.)

AGE. A young pony, like any young animal, is full of joy and mischief. Later on, when you have had the experience of caring for and riding a pony alone, you may want to take on the challenge of breaking or schooling a youngster, but your first pony is not the one for this. Try to find a pony who is at least five years old; six or seven is even better.

It is best not to buy a pony over fourteen years old, though there can be individual exceptions to this, as there can be to any rule. Be sure to ask the vet to check the pony's age during his examination.

TAKING THE PONY HOME ON TRIAL. Occasionally it can be arranged for you to take the pony home for a week or two before you make up your mind about him. But do not be disappointed if the owner does not agree to this. If he lets his ponies go on trial with strangers, he takes the chance that his ponies may return poorly fed, badly cared for, or full of bad habits which may take weeks of schooling to correct before the ponies are fit to be shown to anyone else.

Keep in mind, too, that caring for someone else's pony is an enormous responsibility for you to undertake. Taking a pony on trial is seldom worth the risk.

PONIES FOR THE VERY YOUNG RIDER. It may be that you and your family are looking for a pony for a younger sister or brother

THIS PONY IS A GOOD MOUNT FOR AN EXPERIENCED RIDER

—a pony to keep at home just for fun, so the young member of the family may sit on the pony's back occasionally, pat him, and get used to having the pony close by.

Choose such a pony with extreme care. Too often there is the feeling that "just any old pony will do." Usually it is decided to get a very small one, with the dear little face and innocent expression which most small ponies have. Behind this "sugar cooky" appearance, however, most of these small ponies have clever minds and a sense of mischief which can lead to real meanness. And mean ponies are dangerous, no matter how tiny they may be.

It is better to get a larger and more dependable pony, even for a very small child.

—YET WELL-MANNERED ENOUGH FOR ANY BEGINNER TO RIDE

Handling

As you work with your pony day by day, insist, kindly but firmly, that he do as he is told. He is likely to be a rather shy and timid creature, in spite of his size—but, at the same time, he can be willful and clever at getting his own way, even though his own way may not always be good for him. Ponies are full of contradictions!

Ask yourself the *why's* of your pony's behavior. Why, for example, do ponies panic badly when they become tangled in a rope? Because, in their wild state, ponies were hunted animals who depended on flight for safety. If their legs were caught, they could not run from danger. Consequently, ponies are born knowing a rule for survival they can never forget: "If you are trapped so you cannot run, you must struggle to free yourself—or die."

So it is silly to call a pony "stupid" if he panics. He is only following an instinct far older than his companionship with man.

Misbehavior is another matter entirely! Ponies have a stubbornness and a sense of mischief which can make things difficult, unless you remember that a pony can think of only one thing at a time. If that one thought is concentrated on being foolish, switch his attention to something else. If he stubbornly refuses to come along when you ask him to, for instance, there is no use trying to drag him along, since he is stronger than you. Instead, get his head up and turn him in a circle two or three times to distract him.

Usually the pony will become so puzzled, and so interested in your strange behavior, that he will completely forget what it was he was being stubborn about, and go along with you cheerfully.

Use your imagination and common sense in handling your pony. He may be stronger than you, but you are smarter than he is, and this makes all the difference!

For daily handling of your pony in the stall and paddock you will need a *halter* which fits him well. Good halters are made of leather. (Some halters are made of rope, but these chafe and rub

IF A PONY REFUSES TO OBEY—

DISTRACT HIS ATTENTION, AND—

—THIS USUALLY WILL MAKE HIM FORGET HIS STUBBORNNESS

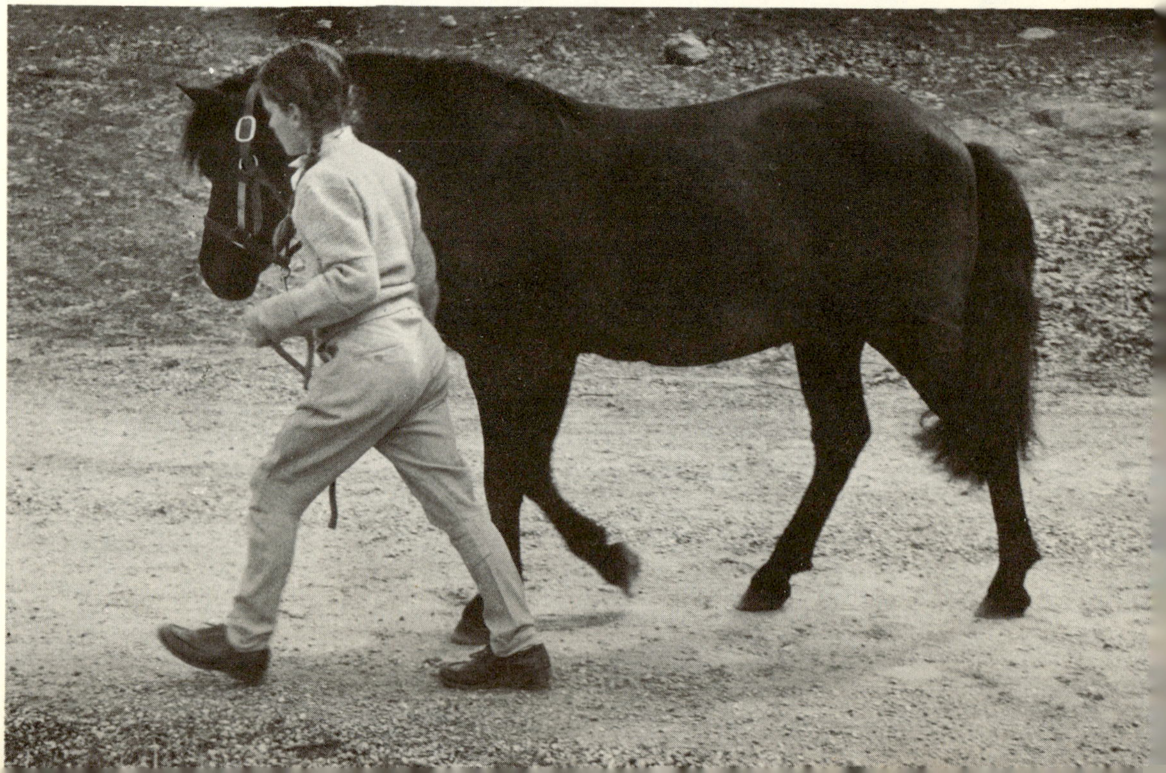

COTTON LEAD ROPE

HALTER

unpleasantly, and they can cause rope burns if the pony pulls against them.)

The halter should fit so that the nose band is held above the muzzle and just loose enough to allow the pony to eat comfortably. The strap which goes behind the jaw should not be so tight that your pony cannot graze or move his head comfortably, nor so loose that it droops away from his head.

As well as a good halter, you will need two good-quality, short cotton lead ropes which are especially made for horses and ponies. These ropes are strong, and they are soft and thick to make them comfortable to hold. Never try to lead or handle a pony by a chain or by a thin or rough rope. If he pulls against these your hands may be cut or burned.

TO LEAD A PONY WITH A BRIDLE OR HALTER. Walk beside him, always on the left, at his head and shoulder. With your right hand, hold the reins close by the bit, or the lead rope close by the halter. The ends of the reins are held in the left hand.

LEADING BY THE REINS
(OR LEAD ROPE)

Do not let the ends of the reins or rope hang too low, or trail on the ground, where you or your pony might trip over them. Hold the free ends folded in your left hand, not wrapped around it.

TO LEAD A PONY WITHOUT BRIDLE OR HALTER. A lead rope, a stirrup leather, or even your belt, may be used to lead a pony in an emergency. Place the rope or strap well up behind the pony's ears and hold the free ends snugly under his jaw with your right hand. Place your left hand firmly on his muzzle, just above the nostrils. In this way you can lead him forward with your right hand, and steady, control, and guide him with your left.

Another method is to hold his forelock in your right hand, using the left hand as I have just described. This method gives very little control, however, unless the pony is exceptionally obedient.

TO LEAD A PONY WHERE HE DOES NOT WANT TO GO. In the picture on the following page, the boy is demonstrating what happens when you try to drag a pony somewhere he does not want to go. If your pony is anxious or suspicious about a strange situation, you must handle him with tact.

First, he must be able to see where he is going! If his head is pulled high or too far forward, he cannot see, and he can hardly be blamed for resisting.

Secondly, facing a pony while you are trying to lead him will almost always stop him in his tracks. Stay back beside his head and

LEADING WITHOUT BRIDLE OR HALTER

shoulder and face forward yourself, or you will only make things more difficult.

Be kind, but firm, with the attitude that he might as well stop his foolishness, because he will have to do what you ask eventually, so he might just as well do it now. *Tell* your pony, through your voice and manner, what to do, instead of *asking* him. Uncertainty on your part will only make your pony uncertain, and more sure than ever that he is right to resist.

LEADING BY THE FORELOCK

DO NOT TRY TO DRAG A PONY, LIKE THIS, WHEN HE IS AFRAID. INSTEAD—

TO TIE A PONY. Use only a sturdy leather halter and a strong lead rope to tie your pony. The rope must be tied short enough to prevent the pony from getting his forehoof or leg over it.

Do not tie him to anything but a tree, fence post, rail, or ring that cannot possibly be broken or torn loose should the pony suddenly throw his weight against it. A frightened pony, galloping free, trailing a broken post or rail behind him on the end of his rope, can lead to nothing but disaster.

Using a thin, weak, or frayed tie rope also can have unfortunate results. A pony standing tied has a feeling of security. If he jerks back and his tie rope suddenly snaps, he loses his head. Once running free with the dangling end of a broken rope swinging from his halter, he may work himself up into such a state of fright that it becomes quite a problem to catch him before he hurts himself.

Never tie a pony by his bridle reins or by a rope snapped to his bit. If he pulls back he may hurt his mouth badly, or break his bridle. If you want to tie your pony up after he has been bridled, slip his halter on over the bridle. Never tie a pony by a rope around his neck.

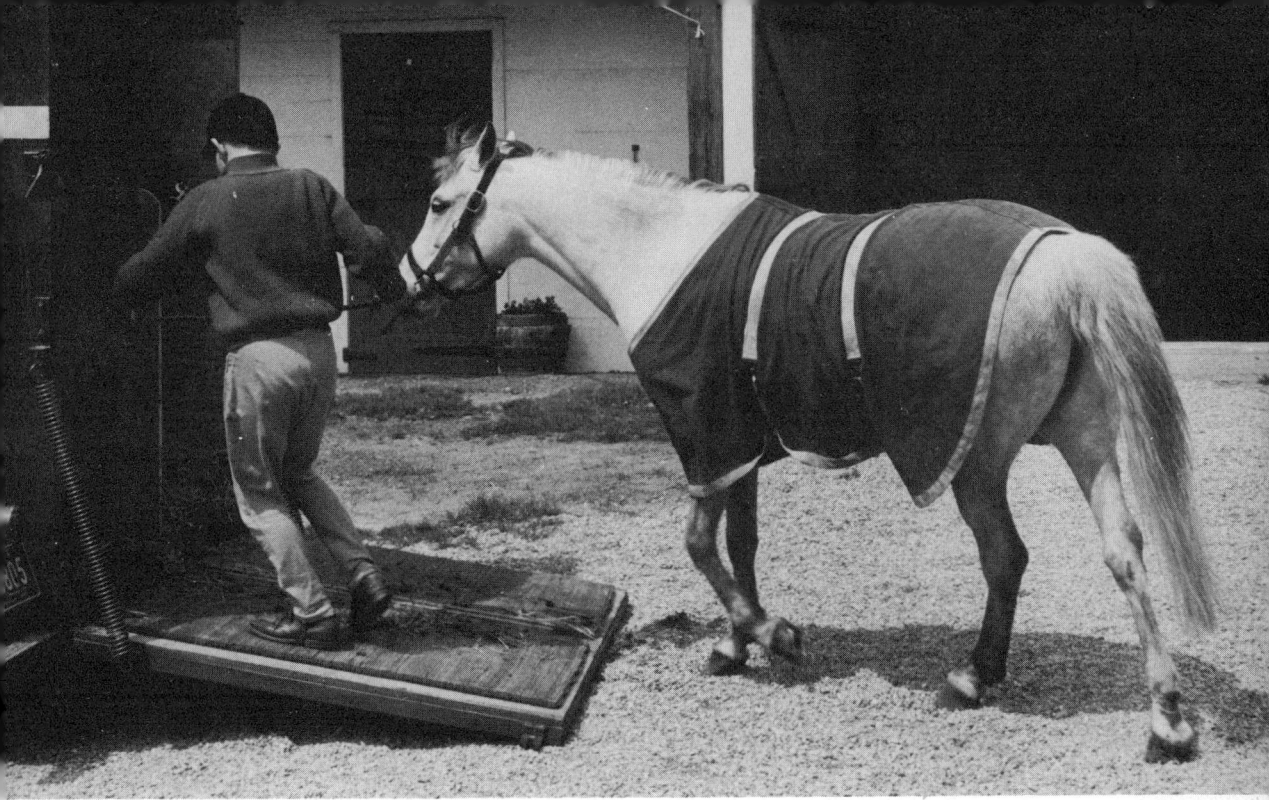

—STAY BY HIS HEAD AND LEAD HIM ALONG QUIETLY; LET HIM SEE WHERE HE IS GOING

TURNING A PONY LOOSE IN A PASTURE OR PADDOCK. **Many ponies greet freedom with a plunge and a happy kick in the air. To avoid a struggle to hold him as you go through the gate, lead him through it slowly and quietly, and turn the pony to face you, before unsnapping the lead rope. Step back and away from the pony as soon as he is free.**

CATCHING A PONY. **Never chase him! Instead, walk toward him slowly with an oat measure in your outstretched hand, where he can see it plainly. Rattle the oats lightly in the measure. Ponies are greedy, and very often they will leave their grass and freedom just for a handful of oats.**

If you are carrying a bridle or rope, hide it behind your back. Your pony may reconsider allowing himself to be caught if he thinks he may have to go to work!

It is easy to teach a pony to come when he is called. Use a special whistle or call each time you want him. Before long he will recognize your call and come to you for his reward, so you must be sure never to trick him; always have a tidbit of some kind for him when he comes.

[23]

LEADING THROUGH A DOORWAY OR GATE. Remember that your pony has four legs! This is sometimes forgotten and the pony's head and shoulders and forelegs are led carefully through a narrow opening, but the hindquarters and hind legs are ignored. This kind of careless handling often results in the pony's striking his hindquarters or hip sharply against the side of the opening, causing a severe bruise and, sometimes, a permanent lameness. So do not hurry your pony through a narrow gateway. Look back to see that his hindquarters are following his shoulders in a straight line, and be ready to stop him or straighten him if his quarters are too close to either gatepost.

IF YOUR PONY IS HARD TO HOLD OR TO LEAD. If your pony becomes stubborn and refuses to be led, or if he is feeling exceptionally fresh and strong, run the lead rope under the halter on the left, across the top of his nose, and clip it to the ring on the right. When the pony tries to go his own way, give the lead rope a quick, sharp jerk. If this does not work immediately, give the rope several such jerks. If he still persists in his bad manners, turn the rope over to someone stronger than you, and ask him to discipline the pony in the same way.

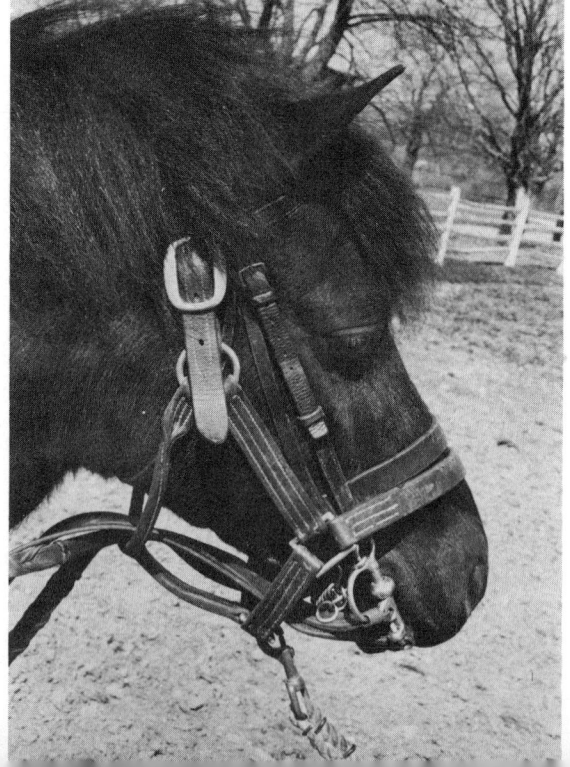

WHEN YOU TIE UP A BRIDLED PONY,
PUT HIS HALTER ON OVER THE BRIDLE

TEACH YOUR PONY TO COME TO YOU WHEN YOU CALL

Once a pony has been made to behave himself, he soon mends his manners, and you will only need to put the lead rope over his nose again to remind him that you will stand for no nonsense.

DO NOT run the lead rope through the pony's mouth, under any circumstances. The burns this causes are a sign of unforgivable cruelty.

Suppose, in spite of your care, your pony should become caught and tangled in a rope, or harness, or bridle, or wire?

Go to his head as quickly as possible, and stay there. This will help calm him, if anything will, and will keep you away from his thrashing legs. Unbuckle, break, or untie any pieces of leather or rope you can reach without leaving his head. If this does not free him, or if it is wire in which he is caught, you must call or wait for help. Push the pony's head down on the ground and keep it there if you can. Stroke and soothe him to keep him from struggling until help comes and he is free again.

GETTING CAST IN THE STALL. Sometimes, when a pony lies down

MAKE SURE THE PONY DOES NOT STRIKE HIS HIP AS YOU LEAD HIM THROUGH A DOOR OR GATE

or rolls in his stall, he gets so close to the wall that he cannot get his legs under his body to get up again. This is called getting "cast." A cast pony may lie still, or he may struggle and thrash wildly.

All that is necessary is to pull him away from the wall. You may need help, however, since even small ponies are heavy. Be ready to jump out of the way as soon as he has been moved, because he will scramble to his feet with a rush the moment he is free.

NERVOUS HABITS

Idleness, boredom, too much confinement, and restlessness from lack of exercise are generally considered to be the causes of nervous habits in ponies, though why some ponies develop these habits, and others do not, remains a mystery. (Unfortunately, other ponies in the stable often learn these habits through imitation.)

CRIBBING OR CRIB BITING. A pony who *cribs* braces his upper front teeth on a fence rail or post—almost any firm surface of suitable height will do—and arches his neck, swallowing a gulp of air with a grunt.

WIND SUCKING achieves the same result, but without the pony's bracing his teeth.

Cribbers and windsuckers usually are more prone to colic than other ponies because of the air they swallow.

WEAVING. A pony who weaves stands facing the doorway or wall of his stall, and shifts his weight from side to side with a rhythmic weaving motion of his head and body.

STALL WALKING. As the name suggests, a pony with this habit moves endlessly around in the stall, or paces back and forth like

ADDED CONTROL FOR A WILLFUL PONY

a lion in a cage.

Weavers and stall walkers wear themselves out. They become thin and drawn from their ceaseless activity no matter how well they are fed.

None of these habits can be cured. Cribbing and wind sucking may be partially discouraged by the use of a *cribbing strap*. This is a broad leather strap which buckles high on a cribber's neck and which is supposed to prevent him from using the muscles of his neck to crib or wind suck, yet still allow him to eat and drink comfortably with his head down. Even under the best of circumstances, however, the cribbing strap does little good other than to make the owner feel he is doing *something* toward preventing his pony from cribbing.

This strap can be used only when the pony is in his stall. It is not safe to turn him out to pasture wearing one of these contraptions, since there is always the danger of his catching it on a branch, fence post, or even on one of his hoofs if he should roll.

Since idleness and boredom have so much to do with these problems, ponies who crib or weave should spend most of their time free in a generous-sized paddock or pasture where there is enough to see and do to keep them interested and content.

VICES

Some things a pony may do are mischievous; others are just plain mean. Improper handling, teasing, or neglect can turn a sweet-tempered pony into a cross one, or a saucy pony into a mean one.

BITING. Most ponies who bite have been encouraged to do so by careless treatment or by teasing.

Do not take tidbits to your pony every time you go near him. He will soon demand them by impatient nipping, which may turn into real biting.

Do not fuss with your pony's head. His muzzle is soft to stroke, but too much of this encourages playful nipping which, again, can turn into real biting. Pat him on the neck or shoulder, instead.

Never tease him by pretending to give him his grain, or an apple or carrot, and then taking it away again. Ponies treated in this manner can hardly be blamed for biting.

If your pony *does* start to nip, slap him sharply on the neck or shoulder and say, "Stop that!" in a very cross voice.

KICKING. This is one of a pony's natural protections and it is his first reaction if he is suddenly startled or frightened. Always move and speak quietly when you are near a pony. Do not touch him on the hindquarters, or walk up behind him, unless you are sure he knows you are there.

Use firm strokes of the brush while grooming your pony. Little, light strokes tickle and may cause some ponies to kick.

Do not run behind a pony, or chase him; this kind of foolishness will make almost any pony kick.

CROWDING. A pony with this unpleasant trick moves his body up against the person in his stall and crowds him to the wall. This does not mean that when a pony bumps up against you because he is impatient for his feed, or has simply moved carelessly, that you must immediately suspect him of crowding. The actions of a crowder are obvious and deliberate. If you keep an eye on such a pony for a day or two, you will soon be able to tell that his actions are not accidental—they have been planned.

If you have determined that the pony is crowding, carry a crop or stick the next time you go into the stall. Keep it hidden by your side where the pony cannot see it. Then, when he pushes up against you, hit him *hard* on his side or rump. Be quick, and be forceful. If you are not strong enough to make this discipline effective, ask someone to do it for you. If crowding is ignored, it can become a dangerous habit; but, if stern measures are taken, crowding can usually be cured.

STRIKING. Some ponies (few of them, fortunately) learn to stand on their hind legs and strike out with their forefeet. Teasing a pony, running in his pasture or paddock and encouraging him to chase you, or chasing him into a corner to catch him—any such silly behavior may teach a pony to strike.

Striking may start through fear, or as a game—whatever the reason, it may become a habit in a surprisingly short time. It is a difficult problem to cure in a pony, so if your pony shows signs of striking, prevent him from doing so in every way you can.

When your pony trots or canters toward you, do not run away, as this will have the same effect as encouraging him to chase you. Instead, stand still, or walk toward him slowly. If it worries you to have him come up to you quickly, stay on the other side of the pasture fence and teach him to come to your call.

Ponies who bite, kick, or strike through real meanness are dangerous. If you are suspicious about your pony's true temperament, ask the advice of an experienced horseman, because a really vicious pony has no place in your stable.

Try not to feel too badly if the pony is so unsuitable that it would be unwise to keep him. There are many, many other ponies who will respond to your care with affection and cheerful obedience; why should you settle for anything less? If you have made a mistake and have bought an unsatisfactory pony, you may comfort yourself with the knowledge that there is not a horseman in the world who has not made the same mistake—and probably more than once!

Stabling and Paddocks

Stabling for your pony need not be elaborate. He requires only a comfortable stall, and you will need a room beside the stall in which to keep grain, hay, bedding, and equipment.

Many tool sheds, storage sheds, and prefabricated garages can be converted into stables. An addition built on the side of a garage can work well (as long as it has a separate entrance for you and your pony), or you can build a separate little stable altogether.

Keeping a pony in a corner of the garage is seldom satisfactory. Garages usually have an unhealthy smell of gas and oil, and most of them are too hot in the summer and too cold in the winter to be good for a pony.

I am taking it for granted that you will give your pony a *box stall*, which, as the name suggests, is a square, or nearly square, stall. In England this kind of stall is called a *loose box*, and this is a very good name for it, since a pony is loose in a stall of this kind and can wander around in it, and lie down comfortably whenever he likes.

The other kind of stall is narrow and is called a *standing*, or *straight* stall. A pony must always be tied in this kind of stall, which makes it difficult for him to lie down, keeps him in the same position for hours, and exposes him constantly to the dangers of tangling a foreleg in the tie rope. Standing stalls are used in big stables only when absolutely necessary to conserve space in a building. There is no reason or excuse for you to keep your pony in such a stall.

A box stall should be at least nine by nine feet square, or ten by twelve feet if your pony is large. This bigger stall has the advantage of being generous enough for a very large pony or a horse. If you are building a new stable, keep this in mind. You will outgrow a small pony eventually and need a bigger one. You might just as well plan ahead.

The height of ceilings and doorways must be generous. It is

THE INSIDE OF THE STALL SHOULD BE LINED WITH SMOOTH BOARDS

interesting to know (and important to remember!) that ponies do not seem to have the sense to duck their heads going through a low doorway. They seldom, if ever, look up over their heads. Many accidents have been caused by a pony's becoming frightened or excited and suddenly throwing his head high and striking it with great force against a too-low ceiling or door.

Insulation is inexpensive and repays its low price a hundred times over by keeping the stall warm and snug in the winter, and cool in summer.

Line the inside of the stall with smooth tongue-in-groove boards. These leave no sharp or uneven edges which a pony can chew or splinter when he gets bored, and they are strong enough to withstand a sharp blow from a hoof.

The floor of the stall should be either earth or clay. Cement and concrete are too hard to be good for a pony's hoofs and legs and, no matter how much bedding you use, somehow a pony manages to scrape and bruise himself on such hard, rough surfaces when he lies down.

If you are converting an old stable or shed that has concrete flooring, the old floor should either be taken up, or covered with wood.

A stall floor of plain earth or clay usually has enough natural drainage. If you find you need better drainage, however, the floor can be dug out about eighteen inches in depth, a layer of stones put down, another layer of smaller stones added, then a layer of cinders, and then it can be finished off on top with a layer of earth or clay.

A Dutch door is excellent for a pony stall. The top half can be left open to give light and air, while the bottom half keeps the pony in the stall. Put *two* bolts on the outside of the lower door: one near the top and the other at the bottom, where the pony cannot possibly reach it. Almost any pony can work a slide bolt easily.

The bottom door should be low enough to allow the pony to get his head over it comfortably.

Try to have this door facing south, with the roof overhanging it. If you can do this, you will find it seldom necessary to close the top door, even in bad weather.

If there is a paddock adjoining the stall so your pony can wander in and out as he likes, be sure the doors cannot swing shut. They must be fastened back *securely*. Use spring snap hooks which are fastened to the doors. These can be clipped into eyes that are screwed into the outside wall of the stall. Unlike plain hooks, spring snaps cannot be shaken loose by the wind. Loose doors which can slam shut are dangerous anywhere in a stable.

If your stall is to have a window, place it, if you can, low enough so your pony can see out of it when he is shut in the stall. Any glass window in a stall must be protected on the *inside* by strong wire mesh. (Fly screening is not strong enough.) Ponies do not understand glass, and your pony may cut himself badly by poking his nose through an unprotected pane.

Use mesh woven widely enough to let your fingers reach through to open and close the window.

Use BX cable if you wire the stable for electricity. Rats often will gnaw through the insulation of regular wire, and this might start a fire.

If you put a light bulb in the stall, it must be placed as high off the ground as possible, and protected by a heavy wire mesh guard, like a strong wire basket. It would be impossible to overemphasize the importance of light bulb protection in the stall. Many dangerous accidents have been caused by a pony's striking his head against an unprotected bulb.

You will need a storage room close to the stall. Hay, grain, and bedding must not be stored outdoors, in a damp place, or on the bare ground. A small storage room built beside the stall is the best answer to this problem.

Clean, new garbage cans, made either of metal or plastic, with tight-fitting lids, keep grain dry and sweet, and protect it from being soiled by rats and mice.

Besides storage space for hay, grain, and bedding, you should have a shelf or box on the wall to hold your grooming equipment

DUTCH DOOR

and first-aid supplies. A few coat hooks will hold your halter, lead ropes, and bridle.

All rakes, pitchforks, brooms, and other equipment must be hung safely off the ground, and must be put back in their proper places immediately after use. Leaving stable equipment lying on the ground or leaning against a fence is carelessness unforgivable around a stable. If you or your pony tripped over a fallen rake or pitchfork, you might easily have an unpleasant—and entirely unnecessary—accident.

Give your pony a paddock adjoining his stall if you possibly can. Freedom from the confinement of a stall means a great deal to a pony. You will find that almost all the year around you can leave the stall door open to let your pony wander in and out as he likes. With an adjoining paddock you need not worry if a sudden storm blows up while you are away from home; your pony can find protection in his stall.

Freedom to move around in a paddock, and to buck and play when he is feeling fresh, helps keep your pony quieter and more pleasant to ride, as well as lessening the problem of full exercise on days when you cannot ride.

A paddock forty by forty feet will give your pony room enough for reasonable freedom. This is the minimum size. You can make it bigger than this if you have the space.

Fences should be approximately four feet high. Ponies are good jumpers and most of them can jump any height less than four feet with ridiculous ease.

Post-and-Rail fencing is safe, strong, and durable. If your pony likes to poke his head through the rails to get at the grass on the far side of the fence, and breaks the rails eventually, or rubs his mane ragged, you can stop this by running heavy wire mesh along the fence. In some neighborhoods trouble can be caused by dogs getting into the paddock and chasing the pony. Wire mesh on the fence and gates will discourage them.

Sheep Hurdle Fencing is attractive and safe but not quite as strong as post and rail. Wire mesh added to hurdle fencing does not spoil its looks and adds to its strength.

Wire Mesh Fencing can be used by itself if it is strong, tightly woven, and made of heavy, smooth wire. Whether used alone or in combination with wooden fencing, the mesh should be small enough to prevent a pony from getting a hoof or leg through it. Some ponies who are spirited and gay or highly bred may not give this type of fencing enough respect. The success you have with wire mesh fencing depends entirely on the pony you want to keep behind it.

Single Wire Strands are dangerous and are not suitable fencing for ponies. Many ponies have been seriously injured by running into wire strands. They are difficult to see and are almost invisible to a frightened or excited pony.

Do not string a strand of wire through a gap in a fence or over a low spot, or to make a fence or wall higher!

Barbed Wire is even more dangerous, if such a thing is possible, than plain single wire strands. Barbs merely add to the damage done

PONIES ENJOY THE FREEDOM OF A PADDOCK ADJOINING THE STALL

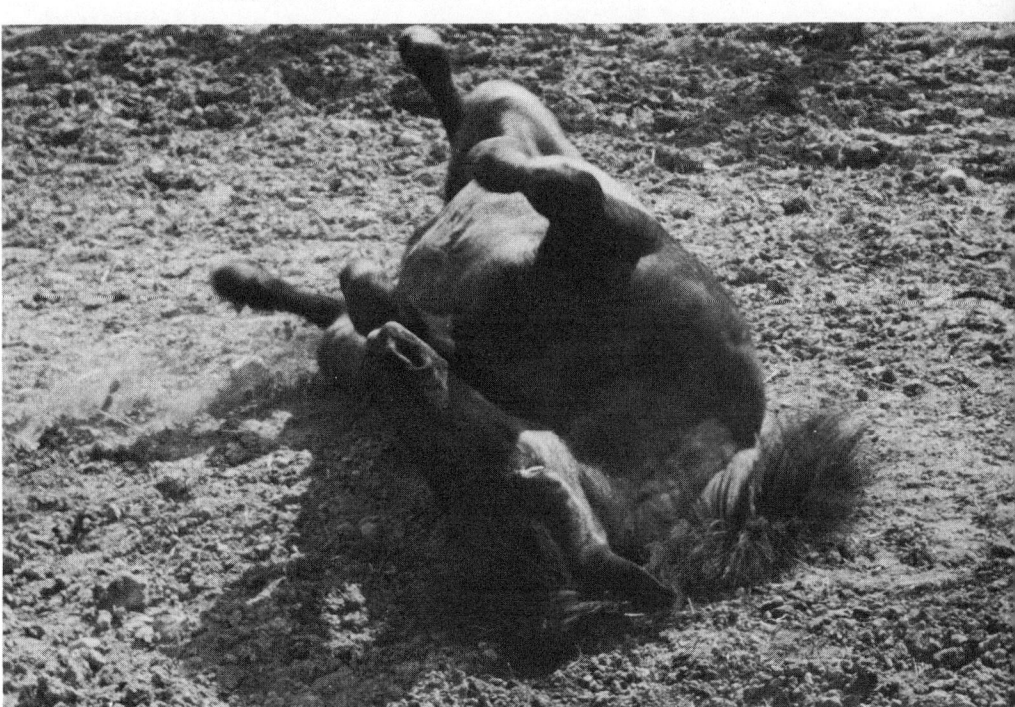

A GATE MUST NEVER BE LOWER THAN THE FENCE.

to the pony if he should become tangled in the wire, or run up against it.

Stone Walls are attractive, sturdy, and safe. Some ponies, however, especially small ones, can climb walls like goats. If you have this trouble with your pony (not all ponies are this agile, fortunately), you may have to run heavy wire mesh against the wall. Or it may be necessary only to add mesh, or a panel or two of post and rail, across particularly inviting places.

Gates must be sturdy, well built, and as high as the fence. (You would be surprised how often three-and-a-half-foot gates are put into four-foot fences, and you can imagine how long it would take a clever pony to find such a pleasingly jumpable spot!)

Sliding bolts are not much use on gates. Ponies soon learn to open them. Use snap catches instead, or a length of chain looped around the gate and post and fastened with a strong, smooth clip.

Whatever type of fencing or gate you use, check all of it carefully for sharp or protruding edges and for free ends of wire (such as those where wire mesh fencing has been cut). These should be firmly looped back on themselves with a pair of pliers.

Make sure all latches, catches, hinges, and bolts are rounded and smooth.

Hammer nails flat or remove them. In other words, try to anticipate accidents before they happen. Do not rely on luck to protect your pony. Protect him with your common sense, instead.

A CHAIN CLIPPED AROUND GATE AND POST PREVENTS ESCAPE

Care of the Stall

BEDDING

Wheat Straw is often used for bedding. It can be bought in bales. It makes a soft, warm bed which is especially nice in cold weather.

Oat Straw can be used as bedding, but most ponies like the taste of it too much, and eat more of it than they should.

The straw you use for your pony's bedding must be bright in color, free from excessive dust, and completely free from a sour smell, dampness, or mould.

Most ponies eat at least a little of their straw bedding, so you must be as particular about the quality of bedding as you are of hay and grain.

Some ponies are so greedy that they will eat a lot of their straw. This stuffs them full of bulk which has no nutritional value, and they soon develop "hay bellies"—fat, swollen stomachs—even though their ribs may show at the same time. Such ponies are much better off on one of the other types of bedding mentioned below.

It takes a generous half-bale of straw to bed down a stall the first time. It is a mistake to think you can save on bedding by using less of it. A skimpy bed gets thoroughly soiled and more of it must be thrown out than with a deep bed, which stays cleaner and fresher much longer.

Break the straw bale apart and shake the straw out into the stall until the bed becomes deep and fluffy. In cold weather, especially at night, bank some bedding around the edge of the stall to help keep out the cold which seeps in at floor level.

Peat Moss bedding stays sweet and fresh a long time. It makes a soft, comfortable bed and is not eaten by even the greediest of ponies.

Though a bale of peat moss is more expensive than a bale of straw, not nearly as much of it must be thrown out each day to keep the stall clean.

A TWO-WHEELED CART IS EASY TO HANDLE

It takes a full bale of peat moss to start a fresh bed—perhaps a little less if your stall is small. Break the clumps with a pitchfork, and rake the bed until it is soft and smooth.

Stable peat moss may be obtained from your regular feed store, or you can get the same type of peat moss from a garden center. The only difference between them is that the garden peat is more easily broken into small pieces; this is of no particular advantage in a stable.

Wood Shavings are good for bedding, and most local mills and lumberyards are glad to let you have all you want just for the asking. Empty grain bags are easy to fill and handle when you go to get the shavings. It takes several bags full to start a fresh bed.

Shavings make a sweet, pleasant bed which ponies will not eat. Be sure to keep an eye out for small pieces of wood or scraps which might have gotten mixed with the shavings at the lumber yard, and which will bruise or cut your pony if he lies on them.

Sugar Cane bought in bales (usually under a trade name) is another good bedding which few ponies will eat.

CARE OF THE STALL

There is no reason for a stall to have a bad smell. Proper care prevents this. Cleaning a stall and keeping it fresh is quite easy, if you go about it the right way.

Once a day give the stall a thorough cleaning. Use a small two-wheeled cart with a handle, for soiled bedding, since the traditional wheelbarrows are clumsy and apt to tip over, and baskets are heavy to carry. Using a four- or five-tined pitchfork, put manure and wet and soiled bedding into the cart. If the bedding is peat moss or shavings, you will need a lightweight shovel as well, since some of the bedding will slip through the fork. Go through *all* the bedding, and be sure to get rid of every bit of it that is soiled.

The more your pony is shut up in his stall, the more cleaning it will need . . . another good reason for a paddock adjoining a stall, though the paddock must be cleaned occasionally, too, of course.

When you are getting the stall ready for the night, tidy it up and add fresh bedding to replace that which has been soiled and taken away during the day.

If there are one or two places in the stall floor which stay damp and smell unpleasant, rake the bedding away from these spots, sprinkle them lightly with garden lime (hydrated lime), and replace the bedding.

Every once in a while, pile all clean bedding in one corner of the stall and sweep the floor with a stiff broom, then sprinkle it lightly with garden lime. If this is done on a bright and breezy day, and you can keep the pony out during the day, leave the bedding in the corner, and let the stall air until you get it ready for the night.

Is all this fuss and bother important? (You may have heard that ponies can sleep standing up, so you may be wondering why it is necessary to keep their beds fresh and clean.)

Ponies *can* sleep standing up, but it is much better for them (and especially for their hoofs and legs) to lie down to rest. Ponies do not like to be dirty, and they do not like to lie down in a damp or dirty stall.

A dirty stall can give your pony *thrush,* which is an unpleasant disease of the hoofs. Thrush is explained fully on page 81.

When you have made a habit of caring for your pony and his stall the way you should, you will find that good care soon becomes so automatic that you will hardly give it a thought—that is, until you go into a stable that hasn't had proper care—and then one sniff, and you will notice the difference right away!

Feeding and Watering

As a general rule, your pony should have all the water he wants, whenever he wants it, winter and summer. There is an old horseman's saying, "Water is your cheapest feed." This simple fact is often overlooked, yet a pony encouraged to drink all the fresh, clean water he needs will have a shinier coat and look and feel better, than the same pony given the same amount of good hay and grain, but watered carelessly.

The easiest thing for you, and the best for your pony, is to keep a bucket of water in his stall where he can reach it whenever he likes.

Some people do not keep water in the stall, but carry a bucket to the pony several times a day, or lead him out to a water tub or a trough. This usually is not a very satisfactory arrangement. It is hard work for you, and a pony is apt to gulp down more water than he really wants or needs, because he knows it may be some time before he gets another chance to drink. On the other hand, if he knows there is water in his stall, he will drink smaller amounts more often, and this is much better for him.

As with any rule, however, there are exceptions—times when your pony *must not be allowed to have all the water he would like to drink*.

Do not give more than a few swallows of water to a hot or tired pony. Let him have three or four sips, then lead him at a quiet walk for five or ten minutes. Let him have another few swallows, then walk him again. Keep this up until he is cool and comfortable and no longer interested in water. Then, and only then, can you safely turn him into his paddock or stall, with his bucket of water where he can reach it.

If your pony is *very* hot, or *very* tired (do not let him get this hot or tired again!) you must take the chill off his water by adding hot water to the cold.

Do not give him all the water he wants if he is extremely thirsty. Too much water all at once is not good for your pony. Though I know you will do all you can not to let this happen, sometimes a water bucket overturns in a paddock, for instance, and by the end of the day you find your pony almost frantic with thirst. At times like this, give him no more than a third of a bucket at a time. Let him wait fifteen or twenty minutes before you let him have a little more. Keep this up until he is satisfied.

Do not let your pony have a great deal of water just after eating grain. (If your pony has had water *before* his grain, as he should have, the few small sips he may take after feeding will not hurt him.)

Water buckets must be kept scrupulously clean. Ponies hate the taste of dirty, scummy, or stale water. They will drink it if they must, but only just enough to take the edge off their thirst. For this reason metal buckets are best for water; they are much easier to clean than wooden buckets, which grow sour very quickly. Plastic buckets are not suitable for feeding or watering, since ponies will chew them and bite pieces from the rims.

Use a handful of earthy grass roots or a twist of hay or straw with a few generous dashes of table salt, to scrub out the water bucket. This combination whisks the bucket clean in a few moments and rinses out well, even when you use cold water. Soaps and household cleansers leave an unpleasant taste clinging to the bucket which your pony will not like.

Give the water bucket this quick scrub once a week. You may find that in very hot weather you will need to do it more often.

Water buckets are heavy. You may find it easier to have two small buckets rather than one big one. Be sure to use buckets with thick round handles because they are more comfortable to carry than the thin-handled ones which cut into your hands.

Hang the bucket (or buckets) up off the floor so your pony cannot tip it over or get his hoof caught in the handle. Use a strong spring snap which is fastened securely to the wall. **Do not use open hooks for any purpose in a pony stall.** Such hooks can tear a pony's muzzle or cut his face badly.

THE WATER BUCKET SHOULD BE HUNG WELL OFF THE GROUND ON A STRONG SPRING SNAP

If your pony is out to pasture a great deal, make sure his water supply is good. Most pasture ponds or streams become stagnant and unpleasant at some time during the year. If the water does not flow freely, and if it is not always fresh and clean, you will have to find some way to keep good water available.

How much water your pony will drink depends on such various factors as the season of year, the weather, the amount of work he is asked to do, or the amount of fresh grass he eats (as opposed to dry hay). In other words, only your own individual pony can be the judge of how much water he needs from day to day.

FEEDING

GRASS can be overrated as a complete food for ponies, though this varies somewhat with the amount of work you want your pony to do. A grass-fed pony will get tired quickly, sweat easily, and will not be up to fast or steady work. But a pony kept for very young children, and not asked to do much more than be led about with a child on its back, may do well on grass alone, *if the grass is of good quality*.

JUDGING THE PROPER AMOUNT TO FEED A PONY IS AN IMPORTANT PART OF HIS CARE

In most parts of the country, pasture varies from season to season. It is apt to lose most of its nutritional value during the hot summer months, and then, in cold weather, it may dry up and be worthless as food. So unless you live where pasture is good at all times of the year, you must plan to give your pony supplementary feeding—good hay, at least, and perhaps some grain.

This does not mean that grass is not good for your pony, but you can let him have all the grass he needs by grazing him occasionally on the end of a lead rope.

Do not feed your pony grass clippings from a lawn mower. These clippings sour very quickly and may give him colic.

NEVER TIE YOUR PONY OUT TO GRASS AT THE END OF A ROPE. This is a dangerous thing to do. You can never know at what moment he may get the rope or chain tangled around one of his legs. **Nothing frightens a pony more than the feeling of being trapped and helpless;** nothing is more terrified or unreasonable than a pony caught and in a panic.

I know you have probably seen ponies staked out to grass, but this makes no difference. The people who do this do not know any better and they have been lucky—so far. Do not risk your pony's getting badly hurt, perhaps breaking a leg, just because you have seen someone else do it. It is not worth it.

Hay is the nearest substitute for grass. Good hay is crisp and bright colored, smells sweet, and is free from dust, dampness, or mould. Good hay is usually a mixture of timothy and alfalfa, sometimes with clover added; the biggest part of any good hay mixture should be timothy.

Hay which is dusty, mouldy, sour, or mow burnt will make your pony sick. *Mow burning* shows as dark brown or black streaks in a bale of hay, often in the center, and it is caused by baling hay before it has been properly dried and cured. The moisture still in the hay makes it hot, and "burns" it. Mow-burnt hay smells good and ponies love the taste, so do not rely on your pony to be the judge of what is good for him!

Unless you have a great deal of protected loft space to store loose hay, you will probably find it is more convenient to buy your hay in bales. Be sure to keep hay well protected and up off the ground.

Any hay showing signs of sourness, mow burning, or mould must be discarded. If you buy a bale of hay and find it is mouldy after it has been opened, tell your feed dealer. He should replace it.

Do not use discarded hay for bedding; remember, most ponies eat their bedding.

QUANTITY OF HAY TO FEED. Because ponies graze most of the day in their natural state, some people believe that ponies must have hay where they can reach it whenever they like. But hay is *dried* grass. It is more concentrated because it has far less water in it than

"GRAZING" A PONY ON A LEAD ROPE WILL GIVE HIM ALL THE GRASS HE REALLY NEEDS

grass and so it must be treated as a completely different food.

Most ponies would eat hay all day long if they were given the chance, but you must be firm. Feed your pony the best hay you can get, and no more in one feeding than your pony can clean up in an hour or an hour and a half. Give him this amount twice a day, with perhaps a little extra in the evening to tide him through the night.

The quantity of hay fed, like any feed quantity, may vary a little with each individual pony. A light-bodied, narrow pony may need a little more hay than has just been recommended; a naturally plump, short-barreled pony, a little less.

Do not use one of those wicked iron mangers with bars as a hay manger. Get rid of it if you have one in the stall. These contraptions are dangerous. Many ponies have caught their forelegs through these manger bars while pawing or playing in their stalls, and have hurt themselves badly. Fluff out the hay and pile it in a corner of the stall, right on the floor, instead.

Rope hay nets are no safer than iron mangers in the stall.

GRAINS

Grains are energy foods, and the amount of grain your pony needs depends entirely on the energy he needs. This not only varies from pony to pony, it varies with each pony from day to day.

A small, Shetland type of pony doing little or no work, and given good grass or hay, may not need grain at all.

This same pony, however, if he is exercised every day, may need one dry-quart measure of grain in the morning and one at night.

A medium-sized pony (11.2 to 13.1 hands—and if you are not sure about these terms of measurement you will find them explained on page 109) may need a little grain to look and feel his best, even though he may be asked to do no more than light work. Two or three quarts of grain a day, divided into two feedings, will probably be enough.

The same pony, in steady work and exercised every day, may need from four to six quarts a day to keep him in good condition.

Large ponies, from 13.2 to 14.2 hands, generally need some grain. Six quarts a day (two feedings of three quarts each) usually is enough.

I know you would probably like me to be more specific about quantity, but this is impossible. Some ponies keep fat, fresh, and fit on almost no grain at all; others fall away to nothing without it. Some ponies, when given grain, become so gay and above themselves that they are almost impossible to manage. Others tire quickly

GIVE YOUR PONY HIS HAY BY PILING IT ON THE FLOOR IN A CORNER OF THE STALL

and are dull and uninteresting to ride without it.

How can you tell? You must use your common sense. Feed your pony just enough to keep him well up in flesh and able to do the work you want him to do—and not one grain more. There is a fine line between over- and under-feeding, and it may take you several months to find just the right balance point for your own particular pony. Do not hesitate to ask your veterinarian for advice. He is as interested as you are in having your pony look and feel his best.

Oats are the most commonly fed grain for ponies. They contain the greatest and best-balanced amount of nutrition of all the grain foods.

Whole oat kernels should be plump, clean, and sweet. Cracked or crushed oats (oats which have been run through a machine to split or crush their hard shells) are easier for a pony to digest than whole oats. It is a good idea to feed crushed oats, but only if you buy them from a reputable dealer, since oats of poor quality can be disguised by crushing.

Corn is sometimes fed to ponies. It is a rich, fattening, heating grain and not a suitable feed except as a small supplement mixed with other grains.

Corn on the cob should never be given to your pony. Even a small piece of cob may choke him.

Sweet Feeds are commercial feeds sold under different trade names. They are a mixture of corn, oats, molasses, and linseed meal. They are very rich.

Ponies love the taste of sweet feeds. They are excellent for tempting poor appetites and for adding weight to a thin pony. Mixed half-and-half with oats they are good for ponies in the winter, but as a general rule they are too heating to be fed during the summer.

Bran has little nutritional value by itself, but it is slightly laxative (like fresh grass), and so it is good for ponies in the winter when there is little or no green grass. Bran can be fed dry, mixed in the proportion of one quart of bran to three of oats.

Good bran is dry, flaky, and sweet to smell and taste. Bran tends to sour quickly, so buy it in as small a quantity as possible.

THIS PONY'S SHINING COAT AND GOOD CONDITION REFLECT HIS OWNER'S FINE CARE

Hot Bran Mashes are good for your pony in cold weather. Hot mashes are easy to digest, and they make a nice feed change for your pony. Mashes are especially good for a tired pony.

Because of their laxative qualities, however, bran mashes usually are not fed more than twice a week. Do not "mash" your pony the night before a show or before a long or demanding ride; save it for the next night instead, when your pony is apt to be a little tired anyway, and especially glad to have a nice hot mash for his supper.

TO MAKE A BRAN MASH. Mashes can be made either of bran alone, or of bran mixed with oats, in the proportion of three quarts of bran to two of oats. You can feed a quart or two more of mash than the quantity you usually give your pony in one regular feeding.

(If you give him three quarts of grain in one feeding, for example, he can have five quarts of hot mash.)

Put the bran or oat-and-bran mixture in a metal pail; add a heaping tablespoon of table salt. (A few carrots, cut up in *small* pieces, are good in a mash, but they are not essential.)

Add very hot water (boiling, if possible) and stir it into the bran until the mash is soft and moist, but not runny or soupy. A short piece of broomstick or a heavy wooden spoon should be used to mix the mash, since the water you use should be too hot for your hand.

Cover the bucket with old towels or several layers of burlap and let it stand until the mash is cool enough to feed. Be sure to put your hand all the way into the center of the mash before you give it to your pony; it may be cool on the outside, but still too hot in the middle! A mash should be fed warm, but not hot. Stir the mash occasionally if you want to hurry the cooling.

Grains and mashes should be given to your pony in metal tubs, or pails, with handles, which can be fastened to the wall with spring snaps.

Make sure there are no sharp edges on your buckets.

Heavy iron grain mangers which bolt into the corner of a stall belong with iron hay mangers—on the scrap heap! They are unsuitable for two reasons: First, ponies can roll or lie down in the stall and get themselves trapped under these mangers. Second, iron mangers cannot be cleaned or emptied properly, leaving grain or mash to turn sour and mouldy. Feed buckets, like water buckets, must be kept clean.

Salt is essential to your pony's health. He must have salt where he can reach it at all times, winter as well as summer.

Bricks of salt, which slip into simple, inexpensive holders, can be bought at any good feed store. Fasten a holder to the wall of your pony's stall four or five feet from the floor.

Your pony will lick the salt brick to get all the salt he needs, but he will not eat more than is good for him.

Salt bricks are made both plain and iodized. Give your pony the plain white salt unless your veterinarian tells you to use the iodized.

FACTS ABOUT FEEDING

Overfeeding grain can make some ponies too fresh and gay, or difficult to handle. If your pony starts to bite, kick, or buck more than usual, try cutting down the amount of grain you have been feeding him.

But semistarvation is not the answer to the question of what to do with a pony too high-spirited for his owner to handle. Experiment with the quantity of grain you are feeding, if your pony begins to give you trouble. But if your pony starts to lose weight, or becomes too listless and quiet, you must increase his grain again immediately and face your problem. Either you need help in learning to handle your pony when he is fit and well, or he is too much pony for you at this time.

BEWARE OF SUDDEN CHANGES OF FEED. Let your pony become used to new feed gradually, and increase *any* food little by little, over a period of several days. Sudden change in feed, or sudden increase in quantity, can give your pony colic. This rule includes grass as well as new kinds of hay or grains. The first grass of spring must be considered a completely new food, since your pony will have been without it all winter long.

How much does it cost to feed a pony? It is impossible to say. Feed costs are determined by too many factors. Prices vary tremendously from one part of the country to another. Ponies out to pasture need less grain and hay than stabled ponies. The size of the pony, the work he is asked to do, the season of the year—all these make a difference in how much food each pony needs. Perhaps you can work out a rough estimate by checking feed prices in your vicinity against the quantities just discussed in this chapter, or perhaps there are pony owners in your neighborhood who can help you answer this question.

Grooming

We usually think of the word "groom" to mean no more than brushing and currying a pony, and keeping him clean. But Webster's unabridged dictionary gives this definition:

GROOM. (v) To attend to the needs of a horse, as by currying, feeding and so forth. 2. To make neat, smart, or tidy.

This definition emphasizes an important point. No amount of scrubbing and polishing the outside of your pony, alone, can give him the shining coat and over-all look of brightness which are the results of good care. Having your pony look his best is like completing a jigsaw puzzle. Giving him clean, sweet water, grain and hay, sensible exercise, a snug, warm bed in the winter, and the coolness of evening pasture in the summer—all of this, combined with all the other details of daily care, work together into a pattern which completes the final picture. In other words, you cannot hide the result of good care. It shows!

However, grooming as we usually think of it—brushing your pony, and keeping him clean—is an important part of over-all care. This is not just for the sake of appearance (though this matters, too). Brisk, thorough grooming rids the pony's coat of dried sweat and dirt, and keeps his skin clean and in good condition. Brushing stimulates the natural oils which keep the coat soft and shining; in the words of an old saying, "One good grooming has the worth of a good feed."

TO GROOM YOUR PONY

To begin with, tie him up with a halter and rope. You cannot do a satisfactory grooming job if the pony is not standing still.

Keep all your grooming equipment in a basket or box which can be easily carried.

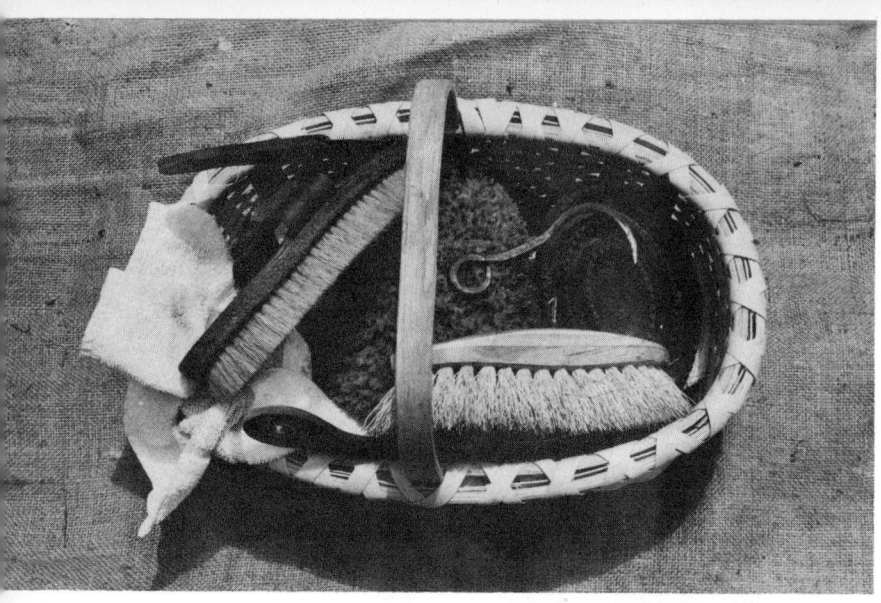

GROOMING BASKET

STAND ON A BUCKET OR BOX TO REACH THE HIGH SPOTS IF YOUR PONY IS TALL

Have a sturdy wooden box or an old bucket to stand on to reach the high spots if your pony is tall.

The Rubber Curry is oval and has blunt teeth, and a web strap on the back through which you can slip your hand. (You may have seen currycombs made of metal, but a metal curry should *never* be

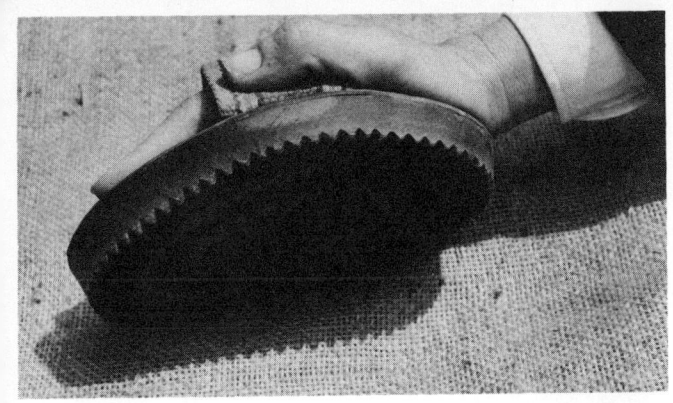

RUBBER CURRY

DANDY BRUSH

used on a pony, since they are so hard they tend to bruise the skin, joints, and tendons.)

The rubber currycomb is used on heavily dirtied spots on your pony's neck or body. (It is never used on a pony's head, or below the knees or hocks, where the bones and tendons are unprotected, and are especially easily bruised.) Curry with a firm, circular motion. When the currycomb gets full of dust, tap it clean against a fence post, wall, or tree.

If your pony has an especially fine coat, or if the coat is short and sleek during the summer, the currycomb may not be needed for every grooming.

The Dandy Brush does most of the grooming. It has a wooden back and long, stiff fiber bristles. It is important to use a brush in good condition. Dandy brushes are not expensive, so when the bristles start to break or wear unevenly, and the efficiency of the brush is lost, it should be replaced.

Start just behind your pony's ears and work back toward his tail.

Brush briskly the way the hair lies and put your weight behind each stroke. Give the brush a flick at the end of the stroke to raise the dust and dirt away from the coat.

The so-called "proper" way to groom is to hold the brush in your left hand while grooming the left, or near, side of the pony, and in the right hand on the far side. I mention this only because I think this rule is nonsense. In the first place, if your hands are small, you may need both hands to hold the brush firmly. In the second place, grooming is hard work, and your hand and arm get tired unless you switch hands occasionally. So hold the brush firmly, but in either or both hands, and go to work.

Brush briskly, but gently, on your pony's knees and legs, to avoid hurting him.

Some ponies like to have their ears and faces brushed with a dandy brush. Be very careful as you brush around your pony's eyes and around the soft, tender skin of his muzzle. If your pony does not like the stiff bristles used on his face, use the soft-bristled body brush intead.

The Body Brush has a leather back with a strap, and has soft, short bristles. Good body brushes are expensive, but unlike the dandy brushes, they last for years.

Hold the body brush in one hand, and the rubber curry in the other. Use the brush in long, sweeping strokes the way the coat lies.

BODY BRUSH

BE VERY GENTLE AS YOU BRUSH YOUR PONY'S FACE

The soft bristles smooth the coat and pick up the dust left on the surface by the dandy brush. After every two or three strokes of the body brush, run the bristles lightly over the rubber curry as it is held, teeth up, in your other hand. This keeps the body brush clean. Tap the dust out of the curry as it collects.

The *Sponges* you use can be either real sponges (which are expensive) or synthetic sponges, which do just as well. Dampen a sponge with water and go over the pony's eyes, the tender skin around the eyes, his muzzle, and the under side of his tail (the *dock*).

There are a few spots which are often missed in grooming. Be sure to pay particular attention to:

The base of the ears.
The hollow between the jaws and the upper part of the throat.
Between and just behind the forelegs.
The inner, upper part of each hind leg.
The backs of the pasterns, and the heels, just above the hoofs.

Ponies of a light color, and ponies spotted with white, may get manure, grass, or mud stains which are difficult to brush out. If the weather is warm, you can wash them out, using warm water and mild soap. Dry the wet patches by rubbing them with a rough towel the way the hair lies. This will keep the coat lying smooth as it dries.

If the weather is cold, but you feel it is really important to get a stain completely clean (such as just before a show), use as little water as possible, do just a small area at a time, and dry the coat as quickly and thoroughly as possible with a towel.

Of course you never groom your pony without caring for his hoofs. This is discussed in the chapter called "Your Pony's Hoofs and Legs."

For a final polish, after everything else is done, go over your pony's coat the way the hair lies, with a soft cloth, to remove the last traces of dust.

CARE OF THE MANE AND TAIL

Mane combs of any kind are useless things which break the hair and make the mane and tail ragged and uneven. Let others buy and use them, if they like. As far as your pony is concerned, the best place for a mane comb is in a wastebasket.

Work snarls and burrs out of the mane and tail with your fingers. It takes years for a full mane and tail to grow, but only a moment to break the hair, so it is worth a few extra minutes to take the tangles out before you start brushing.

Using the stiff-bristled dandy brush, start at the roots of the mane and forelock. Brush every bit, including the under side, even though it does not show!

Use the same brush for the tail. Start at the tip end of the tail and gradually work up toward the dock, so your brush cannot catch in overlooked snarls and break the hair.

During warm weather wash the mane and tail about every six weeks. Use mild soap and warm water and work the suds right to the roots. Rinse thoroughly. (If you would like to, add a little blue-

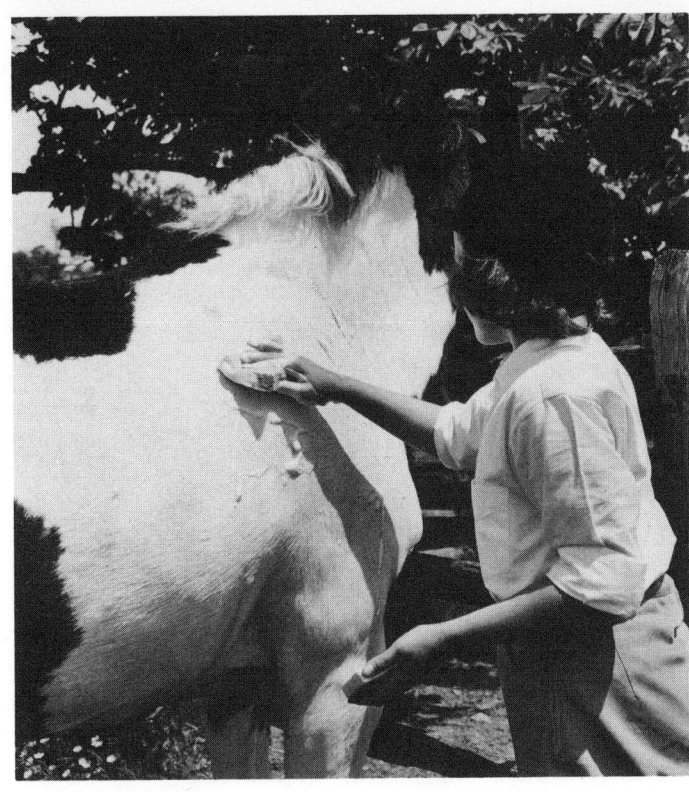

SPONGE OFF STAINS BY USING A MILD SOAP AND WARM WATER

ing to the rinse water if the mane or tail is white or grey). Let them dry completely before you brush them out.

In cold weather, if your pony is used to wearing a blanket, do not let him stand without his blanket while you groom him. Turn the blanket back, and groom his neck, chest, and shoulders. As soon as you are done, replace the blanket and turn the back of the blanket forward to do his body and hindquarters. The mane and tail can be brushed with the blanket in place.

You will find that your pony need not be groomed thoroughly every day. A complete, vigorous grooming once or twice a week will keep your pony's coat in good condition under most circumstances. The rest of the time a brisk brushing before and after a ride (with special attention to where the saddle and girth and bridle lie) and, of course, daily attention to his hoofs, is usually all that is necessary.

"TO KEEP HIM NEAT, SMART, AND TIDY"

There are a few touches which add immeasurably to the smartness of your pony's appearance. They are not an essential part of grooming, but you will be delighted by the difference these few touches make, if you want to have your pony looking his best.

AN OCCASIONAL BATH. You can give your pony an all-over bath if the weather is warm. There must be no cool breeze blowing, and the water you use must be comfortably hot. (*Never* use cold tap water or the garden hose on your pony at any time.) If you are doubtful about the weather, or about the availability of hot water, do not bathe your pony. No bath is worth the risk of having him become chilled.

TO BATHE YOUR PONY: Wash the mane and tail first, then mix up a bucket of hot, soapy water and sponge your pony all over. (Be sure to use a mild soap, since strong soaps or detergents will irritate your pony's skin and dry out his coat unnecessarily.) Rinse him thoroughly with generous amounts of hot water to get all the soap out of his coat. If your pony is gray or has white markings, you can add a little liquid laundry blueing to the final rinse to make the light colors sparkle.

Lead your pony with a halter and rope at a walk until he is dry. If the day is hot and the sun is very strong, walk him in the shade, if possible. Hot, direct sun on a wet coat will make it stand on end. This does not hurt the coat, but it will lose its brightness for two or three days.

TRIMMING. With an electric or hand clipping machine or a pair of scissors with blunt points, trim the long, stiff hair from his muzzle and the shaggy hair from his fetlocks. Trim the small portion of his mane where the halter and bridle lie, just behind the ears; trim this spot as short as you possibly can, but no more than two inches wide, or you will spoil the looks of the mane and forelock.

Never use scissors on the top of the mane, or at the top of the tail, even if you think there are spots that are ragged and need trimming. You will only make things worse. Smooth the ragged spots down with a damp brush, and have patience. They will grow out eventually, which they will *not* do if you cut them.

If your pony's mane stands on end or hangs untidily on both sides of his neck, and you would like it to lie smoothly over on the right side, where it belongs, dampen it thoroughly with a wet brush.

Pull it over to the right and make a single row of tight braids, done up at the ends with small rubber bands.

After three or four days, undo the mane, dampen it again, and rebraid it. Keep this up until the mane stays where it belongs.

(**A note of warning:** The pull of the braids sometimes makes a pony rub the back of his neck against a tree or fence rail. If you see this happening, let the mane stay loose for a day or two, or the pony will break off the top hair of the mane, and it will look worse than it did before!)

Cold and Hot Weather Care

Toward the end of summer ponies start growing their winter coats. By the time cold weather comes their coats are thick and heavy, which brings up the yearly question: Should your pony be clipped?

An unclipped pony gets hot very quickly when he is ridden and it takes a long time for him to cool out. His shaggy coat is difficult to dry once he has begun to sweat, and, since he is especially apt to become chilled during the winter, you must be sure to rub him absolutely dry with rough towels before you put him back in his stall.

Leaving a pony unclipped, however, does have definite advantages. Most unclipped ponies (especially the smaller ones) can go outdoors in all kinds of weather. *This does not mean you can leave your pony out in an unprotected pasture,* but it does mean that you can let him wander in and out of the paddock adjoining his stall all winter long, just as he does in the summer. This freedom helps to solve the most difficult problem of winter: exercise.

School and shorter daylight hours naturally complicate the care of ponies in wintertime. Since daily exercise is essential to your pony, leaving him unclipped and free to go out as he likes to exercise himself in his paddock may be the most sensible thing for you to do.

Do not break your heart trying to keep your unclipped pony as shining and sleek as he is in summer. His winter coat grows oily and rough to help shed rain and snow, and no amount of brushing can make it lie smooth.

When spring comes your pony's coat will shed out in patches, and for a few weeks he will look shabby and untidy. Do not become impatient and decide to clip him at this time! You will spoil the texture of his summer coat if you clip him this late in the season. Go to work on the shedding coat with a rubber currycomb instead, and your pony will soon be sleek and shining again.

If you do a lot of riding every day, a clipped pony is easier to

AN UNCLIPPED PONY CAN EXERCISE IN HIS PADDOCK DURING COLD WEATHER

care for in the winter. He will not get as hot as an unclipped pony, can stand longer and faster work, and is easier to cool out and groom.

A clipped pony has lost his natural protection against cold and bad weather, of course. This means that he cannot be turned out in a paddock for more than a few minutes at a time during the winter, because a clipped pony becomes quickly chilled. Some people turn their ponies out wearing blankets, but I consider this a risky thing to do. Blankets are not made to withstand the pressures of a pony's running, bucking, or rolling in a paddock. If the chest straps break, the blanket will slip, and the pony will become tangled in it.

Since the freedom of a clipped pony is restricted, you must be prepared to exercise him almost every day. A clipped pony requires more care than an unclipped pony, so consider the problems carefully. Once your pony has been clipped, it will be too late to change your mind!

Clipping is done with an electric machine, and these machines are expensive. If there is a riding stable nearby, you might be able to arrange to have your pony clipped there for a fee. If you have a

A CLIPPED PONY HAS LOST THE PROTECTION OF HIS HEAVY WINTER COAT

friend who owns a clipper, perhaps you could borrow it and learn how to use it yourself. Clipping is not difficult, but, as with anything new, it takes a little practice and you should be taught by someone who can help you with your pony and with the clipping at the same time.

If your pony grows a heavy coat, he will probably need to be clipped twice—once in mid-autumn, and again in January. If your pony has a finer coat, wait until late fall, if you can, to clip him, and this one clipping may be enough. It all depends on the individual pony.

Blankets are essential if you live in a cold part of the country and have your pony clipped. Even an unclipped pony may need a blanket, especially at night, and you should have one for him.

A good blanket is made of duck and lined with wool. It has two strong leather straps which buckle across the pony's chest, and two web *surcingles* (broad straps which keep the blanket in place around the pony's body). The blanket should fit snugly and comfortably across the chest and shoulders, cover the pony all the way back to the base of his tail, and be long enough at the sides to keep the pony warm, without being so long that he may kneel or step on it as he lies down.

Cheap pony blankets will turn out to be expensive. They do not wear well, and they do not have enough warmth. Blankets of good quality will last for years.

In very cold weather a clipped pony may need two blankets, wearing one of them during the day, and two at night.

Sheets are unlined duck blankets. They usually have just one strap across the chest, and two surcingles. A sheet serves a number of useful purposes. It can be used to keep your pony clean during the summer when he is in his stall. Putting a sheet on at night at the end of summer, followed as soon as comfortably possible by a blanket, will keep your pony from growing as heavy a winter coat. During the winter it is a good idea to put the sheet on the pony first,

A CLIPPED PONY WILL NEED AT LEAST ONE HEAVY BLANKET WHICH FITS WELL

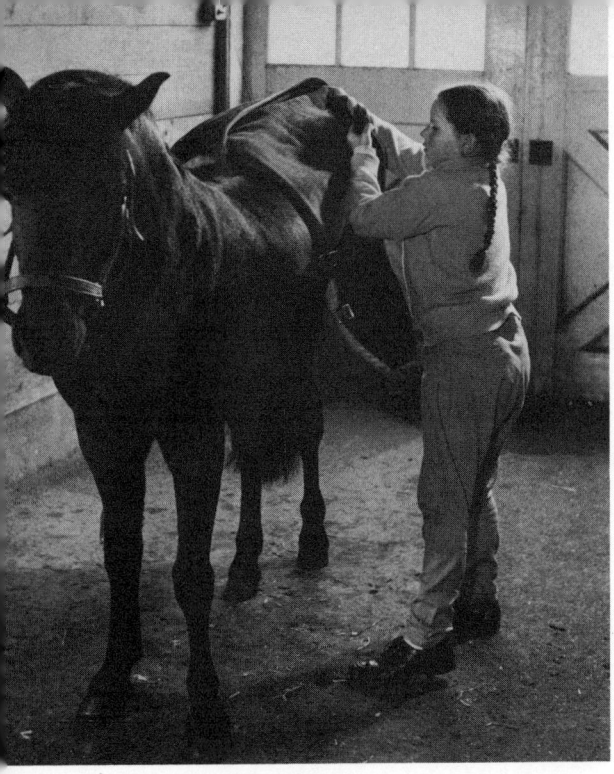

CORRECT WAY TO TAKE OFF A PONY'S BLANKET OR SHEET

before putting on his blanket, or blankets. The sheet makes the coat lie smooth and protects the wool lining of the blanket from the oils and dust in the pony's coat.

When you put a sheet or blanket on your pony, place it well up on his shoulders, buckle the chest straps, then slide the blanket back toward his tail until it is comfortably in place. (This will make his coat lie smooth.) Do up the surcingles and check them to see that they have not slipped and are adjusted to be snug, but not tight.

When you take the sheet or blanket off, undo the surcingles first. Then unbuckle the chest straps and pull the blanket back over the pony's tail.

Never have the surcingles fastened until the chest straps are buckled—not at any time nor for any reason. Suppose the chest buckles were undone while the surcingles were still fastened and your pony made a sudden, quick move. Instead of the blanket's simply sliding off to one side, it would slip back and down over the pony's hindquarters, tangling his legs in the blanket and surcingles.

CARE OF SHEETS AND BLANKETS. Once a week air your sheet and blankets by hanging them over a fence rail and giving them a brisk brushing in the sun and fresh air. Brush the outside of the blanket with the stiff-bristled dandy brush whenever it needs it, leaving it on the pony as you do this, to make it easier.

If you use a sheet under the blanket and brush the outside of the blanket to keep it reasonably tidy, it will probably not need to be washed during the winter. If the sheet needs washing it can go right into the washing machine and be dried and back on the pony by night.

When warm weather comes, wash your blankets in cool water either in a machine or by hand. Since they are lined with wool, it is better not to put them in a drier but to hang them outdoors to dry, instead. Put them away in moth balls for the summer.

HOT WEATHER CARE

It is pathetic to see a pony in a pasture on a hot day in summer, shaking his head, stamping his feet, lashing his tail, and snapping at flies. Too tormented to eat or rest properly, the pony loses weight and becomes cross and miserable.

Flies can be a problem during spring and summer, but they need not drive your pony to desperation. If you have a pasture, of course you want to use it, but instead of turning your pony out during the day turn him out at night. Let him spend the daylight hours in the cool, dim light of his stall, where few flies will go.

Be sure your manure pile is well away from the stable.

Be careful working around your pony when the flies are bad. He may snap or kick at a fly and accidentally strike you instead.

If flies are very bad where you live, you may want to screen your pony's stall. Tack fly screening on the outside of the stall window. Have a lightweight but sturdy wooden frame made to fit the top half of the Dutch door. Cover it on the outside with fly screening, and put strong wire mesh on the inside, so your pony cannot poke his nose through the screen.

This frame can either be hinged or hung from the top on storm-window hooks. One or two small slide bolts (on the outside, where the pony cannot reach them, of course) will keep it snugly in place.

EARLY MORNING IS THE MOST PLEASANT TIME OF DAY TO RIDE DURING HOT WEATHER

Ponies can get heatstroke and sunstroke, just as people can, so try to plan your summer rides during the fresh coolness of early morning or evening. *Be sure your pony can always find shade in his paddock or pasture.* Do not tie your pony, or hold him, in the sun for any length of time; in other words, show him the same consideration you would want for yourself on a hot day.

SWEAT SCRAPER

USING A SWEAT SCRAPER

Even though you try to bring your pony home from a ride dry and well cooled out, you may find, in hot weather, that a film of sweat still clings to his coat. This sticky sweat is hard to brush off even when it is dry, yet leaving it on your pony will make him itchy and uncomfortable.

To make your own work easier, as well as making your pony more comfortable, sponge him off after a ride with very warm water, paying particular attention to the soft skin around his muzzle and eyes, the cleft between his jaws, around the base of his ears, where the saddle and girth have been, and between his hind legs. If he has been very sweaty, you may want to sponge him all over.

NEVER, NEVER USE COLD WATER ON YOUR PONY. No matter how sorry for him you may feel on a scorching summer day, sponging him with cool or cold water (and this includes the water from the garden hose!) will make him very sick, perhaps even cripple him for life. (See *Founder,* page 93.)

A Sweat Scraper is not a necessity, but it is a convenience. It is made of flexible metal, with a wooden or leather handle at each end. After a pony has been washed or sponged, take a handle in each hand and draw the scraper along the pony's coat the way the hair lies. This presses most of the water out of the coat, and the pony will dry in a much shorter time.

After a few moments of experimenting you will find how much pressure to use to get the most water from the coat without hurting the pony. The scraper must never be used on a pony's head, or over his knees, hocks, and legs.

Your Pony's Hoofs and Legs

A pony's hoof is like a box. The outside is made of insensitive horn (similar to your fingernails), and it is lined inside with a soft, sensitive tissue called the *lamina*. In the center of the hoof are the small, delicately balanced bones which bear your pony's weight.

The bottom of the hoof is slightly cupped. When you pick up a pony's hoof you see the *frog*, which is V-shaped, sturdy, and elastic, and acts as a shock absorber when the hoof strikes the ground.

The horn of a pony's hoof grows constantly, as your fingernails do. It is absolutely essential that your pony's hoofs be cared for by a good blacksmith every four to six weeks, whether or not your pony wears shoes and whether or not he is ridden.

The blacksmith will trim and shape the hoofs to keep them in balance, so they bear the pony's weight evenly, and keep the pressure of the frog on the ground as it should be.

If this trimming is not done regularly, the pony's hoofs will grow so long that the heel will contract and the toes may chip, crack, or break, whether or not the pony is wearing shoes. A small split in the hoof can make a pony lame, and takes a long time to heal.

Neglected hoofs may make your pony stumble and, under any circumstances, the legs and hoofs will be thrown off balance, straining all the muscles and tendons of the legs.

No hoof, no horse.

A horse is no better than his hoofs and legs.

These two old and familiar sayings help to emphasize the tremendous importance of proper hoof care. It would be well for you to remember them.

Whether or not your pony needs to wear shoes depends entirely on the individual pony and the work he is asked to do. The hoofs of some ponies are tough enough to do very well without shoes. Ponies which are ridden mostly on dirt roads or fields may not need shoes either. Shoes are worn to protect the hoof from wear, especially from uneven wear, and from being cracked, chipped, or broken on hard roads or stones.

Watch your pony's hoofs carefully if he is not wearing shoes. If a hoof starts showing signs of uneven wear, or of chipping or cracking, you will see these warnings of trouble in time and can have the pony shod before the hoof is badly damaged or he goes lame.

White hoofs are softer than dark ones.

If you do not know of a good blacksmith, ask your veterinarian or a nearby riding stable to recommend one.

If your pony's shoes are not worn down at the end of the month, the blacksmith will take them off, trim the hoofs, and replace the same shoes.

If your pony stumbles frequently, strikes one leg with another, or clicks the front of a hind hoof against a forehoof as he trots (this is called *forging*), tell your blacksmith the next time the pony is shod. The blacksmith may be able to balance the shoes in a different way to help solve these problems. A good blacksmith is a craftsman, and his knowledge and skill can make a great difference in the way your pony moves.

SHOEING BALANCES THE PONY'S HOOFS AND PROTECTS THEM FROM CHIPPING OR BREAKING

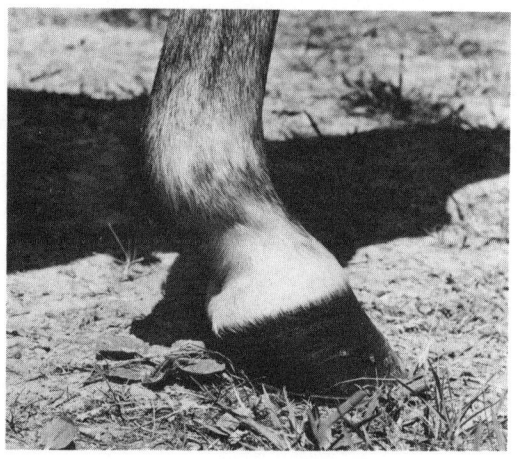

Frequent stumbling can also be a sign of lameness. If your blacksmith cannot help your pony, you should consult your vet.

Check your pony's hoofs once a day even if you have not ridden, and check them before and after each ride. This takes only a moment, but in this moment you can clean each hoof, see that the shoes are firmly in place, and make sure that nothing is caught inside the hoof which might bruise the sole or frog. Make sure all *clinches* are down (the clinches are the tips of the horseshoe nails which come out about a third of the way up the hoof, and are tapped down against the hoof after the blacksmith has nailed the shoe in place).

A raised clinch is sharp and, if it is on the inside of the hoof, it can cut the opposite leg badly. Tap the clinch down against the hoof gently with a stone or hammer, and remember to call the blacksmith, because raised clinches usually indicate worn shoes.

If your pony should loosen or lose a shoe while you are out riding, ride home slowly and on the soft shoulder of the road.

Occasionally a shoe will pull halfway off. Heavy mud can do this, or the edge of the shoe can catch on the side of a stone—whatever the reason, this leaves the shoe still tightly in place on one part of the hoof, but with the rest of it twisted or bent out of shape, free from the hoof but with the nails still in it.

Fortunately, this does not happen very often, but if it should happen, you have no choice but to pull the shoe right off. Frequently part of the hoof breaks off when you do this, but this is minor damage compared to the risk of having your pony step on the twisted shoe and drive one of its nails deep into the inside of his hoof.

If you live where there is ice and snow in the winter, you may want to have your pony *sharpshod*. This means your blacksmith will put sharp heels or frost nails on the shoes to give the pony a better grip on icy surfaces. Sharpshoeing sometimes has drawbacks, however, since it increases the danger of your pony's *calking* himself (cutting and bruising the opposite leg, usually just above the hoof, with the sharp heel of the shoe). Watch out for calk wounds and clean them thoroughly as you would any wound (see page 96 in

YOUR PONY MAY NEED TO BE SHARP-SHOD IN WINTER

the chapter on First Aid). If your pony calks himself too often, he would be better off without sharp heels.

Some ponies' hoofs become too dry in hot summer weather. Ask your blacksmith about this and he will recommend a good hoof dressing if your pony needs it. You will put the dressing on with a brush once a day.

TO PICK UP A PONY'S HOOF

FOREHOOF: Stand close beside the pony's shoulder, facing his hindquarters. Run your hand firmly down the back of his leg from the knee to the fetlock. If he does not pick up his hoof, lean the weight of your shoulder against his. This will throw his weight onto the opposite leg, and very often this is all that is necessary to overcome his stubbornness. Sometimes moving him forward a step or two will do the trick.

HIND HOOF: Stand close beside his hindquarters, facing the tail. Use the same method as you would for the foreleg.

A pony's legs have no lateral movement. This means that a pony can move his legs forward and back, but not to the side. Do not at any time pull your pony's leg sideways away from his body.

Your pony's hoofs must be cleaned out once a day, *every* day, without fail.

TO CLEAN A PONY'S HOOF: Use only a curved, blunt hoof pick. You can get a hoof pick wherever brushes and other pony equipment are sold, or you can ask your blacksmith to make you one. *Never* use a sharp instrument, such as a screwdriver, instead of a proper hoof pick. You might easily cut or bruise the pony's foot.

Pick up the hoof (see page 80) and clean it thoroughly, working from the heel toward the toe.

There is nothing difficult or complicated about picking out a pony's hoof, and the few moments it takes are important in the prevention of a disease of the hoof called *Thrush*.

Thrush is often caused by neglect, by careless and inadequate cleaning of the stall, or by keeping a pony in a paddock or pasture which is wet and muddy.

The disease starts as a slight, damp softness in the cleft of the frog, accompanied by a distinctive and very unpleasant smell. If nothing is done, the dampness turns to an oozing discharge and the whole frog becomes involved.

Unless the thrush is unusually severe, the pony will not be lame, and can be ridden as usual.

Sponging the frog with a strong salt-water solution will help, but the only cure for thrush is to find the cause and correct it.

The *why* of lameness can be difficult to tell, but there is nothing the least bit difficult in knowing *when* a pony is lame.

In the first place, you can *hear* lameness. When a sound pony

PICKING UP A PONY'S HOOF

trots, his hoofs hit the ground squarely with an even one-two-one-two beat. Lameness—even slight lameness—changes this rhythm, since the pony favors the lame leg, hesitates to have it strike the ground, and lifts it up again quickly with each stride. The hoofbeat then changes to an uneven one-TWO, one-TWO.

You can *see* lameness, either on a pony's back or from the ground. When a sound pony trots, he holds his head quite still (it does not bob up and down as it always does at the walk and canter). A lame pony, however, as he trots, lifts his head with one stride and drops it with the next. This is called *nodding*.

If you think your pony might be lame, either ride or lead him at a slow trot along a firm surface. (This is called "jogging for soundness.") The reins or lead rope should be slack. Watch him for nodding and listen for any change in the rhythm of his hoofbeats. Naturally, the lamer the pony, the more these signs will show.

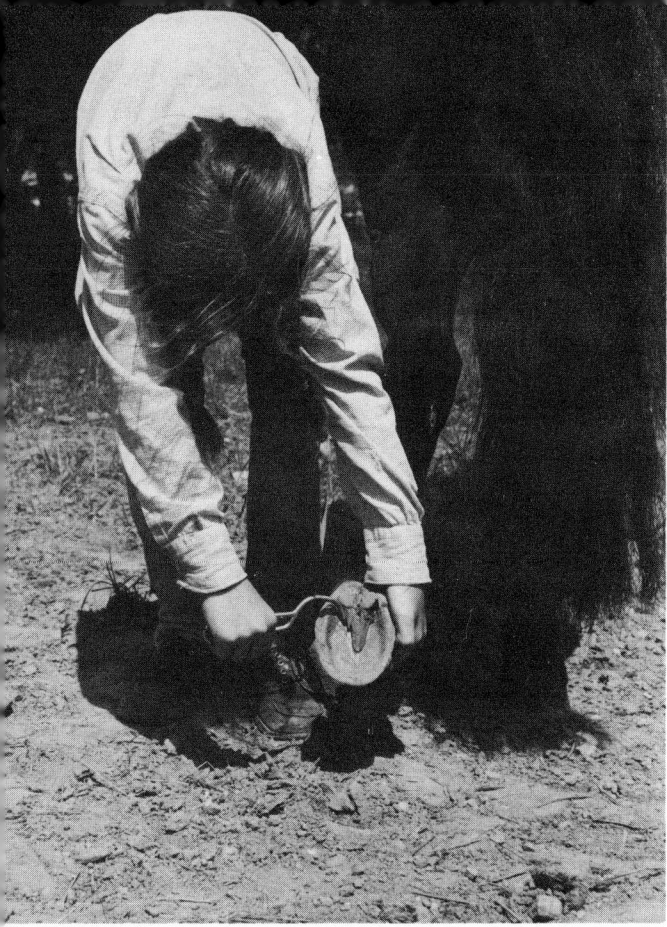

CLEAN YOUR PONY'S HOOFS
WITH A BLUNT HOOF PICK

HOOF PICK

Continually standing with more weight on one foreleg than the other is another sign of lameness. (By far the greatest percentage of lameness is in the forelegs.) The lame pony may stand with one foreleg slightly ahead of the other, or stretched well forward with the fetlock flexed and the toe resting on the ground. This is called "pointing." Or the pony may stand in a more natural position, but observation will show that one leg is always bearing more weight than the other; or the unsound leg may be relaxed and the ankle flexed back, carrying no weight at all.

(It is perfectly natural for a pony to "cock" one hip and rest one hind leg at a time; this is not a sign of lameness.)

Any pony may stumble occasionally, but *frequent* stumbling is a sign that there is something wrong. Either the pony is not properly shod, or he is showing a sign of lameness.

If your pony is lame, you must find out why, though you will need professional help unless it is something very simple, like a stone in his shoe. If the tendons or joints of one leg are just the least bit puffy and swollen, indicating possibly just a slight strain, or if one hoof feels just slightly warmer to your hand than the opposite hoof, give your pony a day of rest. (Be sure to cut his grain feedings down to half the usual amount.)

If the lameness disappears after his rest, work him very lightly for a few days more, and, if he stays sound, then go on as you did before. But if the puffiness or swelling returns, or if they are severe, or there is great heat in one hoof or joint or tendon, or your pony is quite definitely lame (not just a little gimpy), then do not wait. Call your veterinarian. As with any illness, lameness is more quickly and easily cured if it is properly cared for at its start.

If your pony suddenly goes lame while you are out riding, stop, dismount at once, and try to find the trouble. He may have picked up a stone in his foot. If this is the trouble and you cannot get the stone out with your fingers, try prying it out with another stone. If this does not work, lead the pony slowly until you can find someone to help you remove the stone.

Sometimes sudden lameness on a ride is caused by stepping on a sharp stone or by bruising a leg on a tree stump or log. If you dismount and wait a few minutes, the sting of the bruise may go and your pony trot out as sound as ever.

Whatever the reason, during any lameness, stay off your pony's back! Your added weight will not help.

Another cause of sudden lameness is a disease called *azoturia*. The pony starts out for a ride feeling fresh and gay and showing no signs of trouble. Ten to twenty minutes later, he starts to move his hind legs stiffly. If his rider does not notice the change in his gait, and forces the pony to go on, the stiffness in the hind legs turns to severe lameness, then to staggering, until finally the pony falls down and cannot get up again.

Azoturia is caused by overfeeding and lack of exercise. Another name for it is "Monday morning disease" because ponies often were rested on Sundays and taken out to be worked again on Mondays.

JOGGING FOR SOUNDNESS: LEAD THE PONY AT A TROT WITH REINS OR LEAD ROPE SLACK

And azoturia usually appears the day *after* a day of rest.

(You cannot shut your pony up in a stall without exercise. You must remember to cut his grain on days when you cannot ride. I know I have said this before, but it cannot be repeated too often. Colic—founder—azoturia—these are high prices to pay for forgetting this simple rule of pony care.)

A good rider is always aware of his pony's behavior. If you notice your pony suddenly moving his hind legs in a strange manner, stop at once. Usually, if he is having an attack of azoturia, he will break out in a sweat. He may be restless and uneasy, showing symptoms not unlike those of spasmodic colic, but above all, there will be the peculiar stiffness in the hind legs.

Every step a pony takes from the beginning of an attack of azoturia adds to the danger of the disease. You must not try to lead or ride your pony for help. Help must come to him.

Dismount, leave the saddle on, but loosen the girth. If you are wearing a jacket or sweater, take it off and put it over your pony's back just behind the saddle. If you have been riding with a friend, send him to the nearest house to telephone for the vet. If you are alone but near a house or road, call for help. If there is a tree, fence post, or shrub nearby, tie your pony by the bridle reins and go for help.

Not too many years ago an attack of azoturia damaged a pony permanently. Today there are new drugs which, if given to the pony on the spot, without his having been forced to move, can cure him or, at the very least, cause considerable improvement. But remember: It is your observation and knowledge of your pony's normal behavior which can save his life by your noticing the symptoms of azoturia at the very beginning of the attack.

Treat your pony's legs with respect. They are beautifully made and delicately balanced to carry your pony, with you on his back, through years of companionship and pleasure. But misuse and abuse will shorten their usefulness, and so shorten your pony's life, because, once a leg has been damaged, you cannot go out and buy a new one as you can buy a tire for a car.

IF YOUR PONY SUDDENLY GOES LAME, HE MAY HAVE PICKED UP A STONE IN HIS SHOE

Walk your pony for the first ten to fifteen minutes of your ride to loosen his muscles. Trot the next several minutes, then walk again, then canter a bit, slowly, to complete the warming up, before you ask your pony to gallop, jump, or to make quick turns or to exert hard effort of any kind.

Ride at no faster than a slow jog trot on paved roads and over rough or stony ground, because these surfaces increase the force of the concussion of the hoof and leg when they strike the ground. Limit fast paces to soft dirt roads or grassy fields which "give" a little under your pony's weight and help absorb the shock of each stride.

Do not ride fast up or down hill, or through mud.

Do not batter your pony's legs to pieces by long hours of fast riding over ground that is dry and hard in summertime or frozen in the winter. (Riding in the snow is another matter. Snow cushions the ground, and ponies love it!)

Walk your pony the last twenty minutes of your ride to relax him and cool him out before you get home.

GALLOP YOUR PONY ONLY WHERE THE GROUND IS SPRINGY AND FREE FROM HOLES AND STONES

A HEALTHY PONY HAS AN ALERT EXPRESSION, AND HIS EYES ARE BRIGHT

Illness and First Aid

There is a look of brightness about a healthy pony like the glow of a candle in a jack-o'-lantern. A happy, healthy, well-cared-for pony is fun to own, a delight to ride—and a credit to the one who takes care of him.

A pony in top condition has an alert expression. His eyes are bright, and his ears prick up at any interesting sound or sight. He waits anxiously for his food and finishes every grain. His ribs are well covered and his hindquarters rounded without his being fat. Above all, his coat blooms with a soft glow that no amount of grooming can bring out if the pony is not well.

A pony not feeling his best tells you in a number of ways. His coat, instead of lying flat and close to his skin, stands out roughly

A SICK PONY LOOKS MISERABLE, AND HIS EYES AND EXPRESSION ARE DULL

and loses much of its shine. His skin may look as though it has been pulled too tightly over his body (this is called being "hidebound"). He may be droopy and have a dull expression.

A really sick pony stands in a miserable heap. He may not be as hungry as usual, or he may lose his appetite altogether. (If a pony who usually eats well begins to turn away from his grain before it is finished, or refuses it altogether, you may be sure there is something wrong!) A sick pony may lie down more than usual, or he may be unwilling to lie down at all.

You may have heard that you can tell if a pony has a fever by feeling his ears. This is not true. A pony's ears (and his legs, as well) can be icily cold at the same time that he is running a high fever.

Teeth which have not had proper care can keep your pony from looking and feeling his best. Ponies wear their teeth down unevenly as they eat, until they become so rough and sharp that they cut the sides of the mouth and tongue, well toward the back, where it does

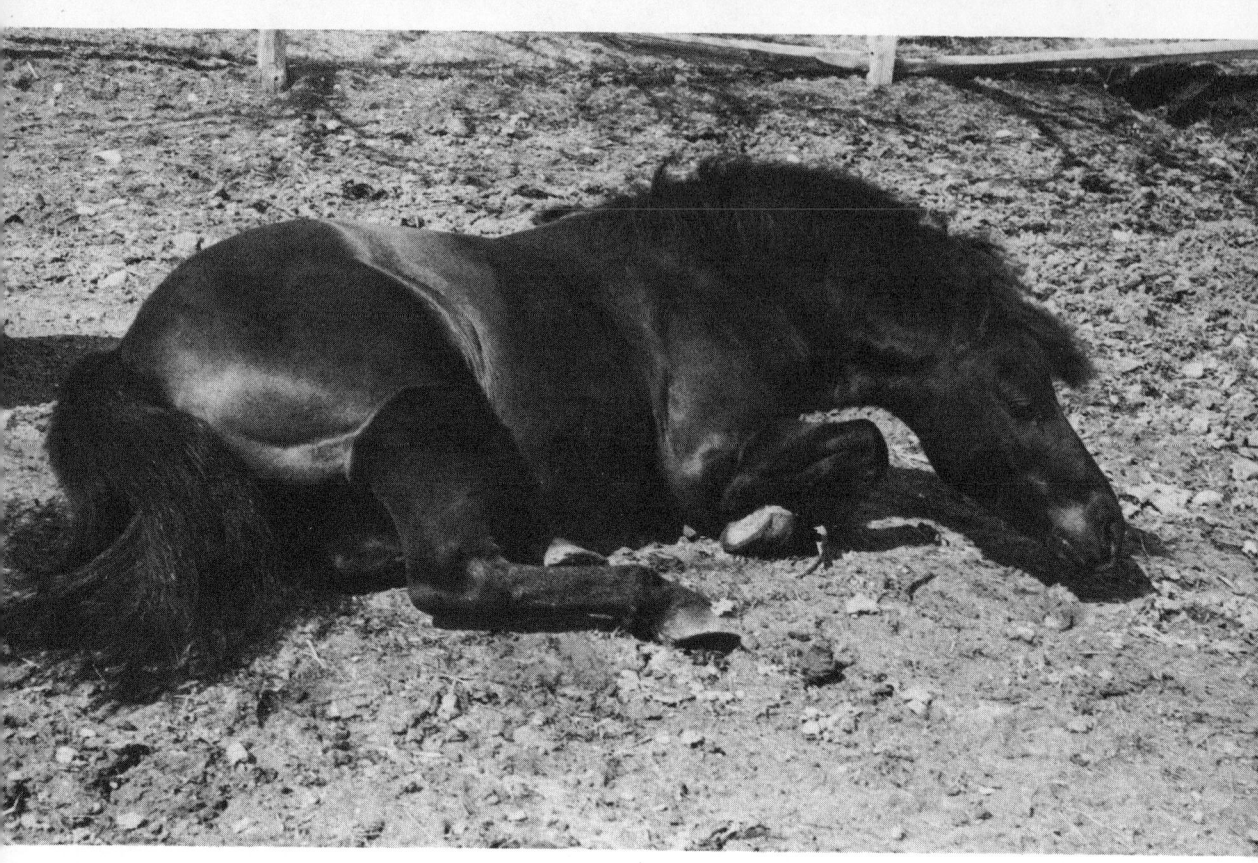

A SICK PONY MAY LIE DOWN MORE THAN USUAL, OR HE MAY NOT LIE DOWN AT ALL

not show. If your pony's teeth are rough he cannot chew properly and he will get little good from his food.

Once every year you should have your pony's teeth checked by your vet. If the teeth need care the vet will "float" them—smooth them with a special rasp—until they are even and meet properly. This does not hurt the pony in the least.

Worms can also cause general "unthriftiness," because they can be responsible, too, for your pony's not getting the good he should from his food. Your pony can look reasonably well, but still have a light case of worms. Once a year, as a matter of course, have your vet check your pony for worms. Though you cannot prevent them, you can do something about them, and do it before they cause much harm. It is such a waste of time and money to feed a pony well, and ignore the fact that poor teeth, or worms, can be wasting so much of his food!

A severe case of worms causes a dry, harsh coat, a bloated stomach, dull eyes, and dull expression. Sometimes a pony with worms will rub his tail against a tree, fence post, or rail. Ponies with worms (or, again, poor teeth) may eat strange things like earth, manure, or bark from trees. These poor creatures are trying to replace the vitamins and minerals which they need so badly but are not getting from their food.

Any time you are responsible for the care of a new pony, have his teeth checked and have him tested for worms right at the start.

COUGHS. A perfectly healthy pony may cough occasionally to clear his throat of dust, a bit of hay, or anything else which may be irritating. Frequent or prolonged coughing is a different matter altogether and should not be ignored.

A condition called *heaves* can cause frequent coughing. A pony can get the heaves from eating feed that is of poor quality, or that is dusty, mouldy, or sour. The elasticity of the lungs is affected and the pony develops a deep cough. Though heaves cannot be cured, this condition can be helped if the vet is called at the start, and the pony may be able to continue in a happy, useful life.

A *cold* can give a pony a cough, as can any illness which starts with coldlike symptoms. Whether or not he has started to cough, a pony with a cold has a runny nose and weepy eyes and feels miserable. Sometimes the glands behind his jaws are swollen.

Be sure to call the vet if your pony shows signs of a cold. It may be no more than a sniffle, or it may be the beginning of an illness which, if it is not treated promptly, can become dangerously severe.

Never ride a pony with a cough or cold, unless you have specific instructions from your vet.

Colic is a word which covers all kinds of stomach-aches in ponies. There is no such thing as a "slight case of colic." A pony either has colic, or he does not have colic. And if he does have colic, he needs a vet just as quickly as possible.

Ponies cannot vomit. If they eat something which is bad for them they cannot be sick as most other animals can. This is why you must be so very careful with everything your pony eats.

Colic can be caused by any sudden change in feed, too much feed of any kind at one time, drinking water after eating grain, eating mouldy, sour, or poor-quality grain or hay—in other words, colic can be caused by anything which your common sense tells you could give your pony a stomach-ache.

A favorite, and dangerous, trick of ponies is to escape from their stalls or paddocks, if they possibly can, and eat themselves sick on anything they can find. This includes such things as too many apples in an orchard, too much of any growing crop (such as corn), or getting into the grain or bran and eating all they can hold. If you find your pony in such a situation, shut him up in his stall, *do not let him have any water,* and call the vet *at once.* Do not wait for colicky symptoms to show. Colic is almost invariably the result of such escapades.

The symptoms of colic depend on whether your pony has *spasmodic colic,* which causes a sharp, painful stomach-ache, or *flatulent colic,* in which the pony is so swollen up inside he can hardly breathe.

With *spasmodic colic,* the pony may turn his head to look at his stomach and sometimes poke it with his nose. He may paw the ground, or walk around uneasily. When the pain goes for a short while, he may go back to his grain or hay, but he will stop eating when the pain returns. He may kick at his stomach, or switch his tail crossly, and may break out in a sweat.

As the pain increases he may lie down and roll, get to his feet, then go down and roll again.

With *flatulent colic,* instead of becoming restless, the pony becomes too quiet. He stands with an anxious expression, often with his ears turned back as though listening to the pain in his stomach. He may lie down carefully every now and then, as though trying to find a position which somehow will lessen the pain. He may breathe unevenly, with his nostrils flared, and may break out in a sweat. His stomach may be greatly swollen.

If you find your pony showing symptoms of colic, take away all feed and water, and call the vet at once.

FOUNDER. Founder causes the tissue inside the hoofs to swell. Since the outside of the hoof is hard, the swelling has nowhere to go and the pressure inside the hoof builds up until it causes intense pain.

Any of the causes of colic can also be a cause of founder. This disease also can be the result of riding a pony to the point of exhaustion or working an unfit pony at fast speeds, or riding too fast or too long on hard surfaces.

ONLY A VETERINARIAN'S EXAMINATION CAN TELL HOW SICK A PONY MAY BE

TURN YOUR PONY OUT, IF YOU CAN, ON DAYS YOU CANNOT RIDE

Sudden chilling can founder a pony. This is why you must never give a hot pony cold water to drink, sponge him off with cold water, or let him stand with a cool breeze blowing on him when he is warm from exercise. A pony who is hot from being ridden can founder on a cool day just by being allowed to stand still. Keep your pony walking quietly until he is absolutely cool and breathing normally.

Founder can also be caused by overfeeding and lack of exercise. A common cause is keeping a pony shut up in a stall without exercise, and the danger is greatly increased if the owner forgets to cut down the pony's grain to no more than half his usual amount. Grain feedings must be cut *whenever* the pony gets less than his usual amount of exercise. Usually only the forehoofs are affected, and they become unbelievably hot to the touch.

A foundered pony may rest his head on a stall door, or a fence rail, to help take the weight off his hoofs. He can barely manage to walk and he should not be made to do so. He will run a high fever, usually accompanied by heavy sweating.

If you suspect your pony may be having an attack of founder, take away his feed and water and call the vet at once. The sooner the pony is treated, the better his chances of recovery without severe and permanent damage to his hoofs.

I have discussed these few illnesses thoroughly so you might understand how many cases of heaves, colic, and founder can be prevented by thoughtful care and attention to a pony's needs. But this is not a book of veterinary care. It is not the place of a pony owner

to diagnose his pony's illnesses—only to prevent them, as much as is humanly possible, through knowledge and thought and good care.

But it *is* the owner's responsibility to watch his pony intelligently, have the sense to become suspicious when his pony's manners or actions change to any unusual degree, and to call his veterinarian at the first signs of trouble. The fee your vet will charge will be small compared to a long, anxious battle to save your pony's life, which may very well be the case if you should wait too long.

EUTHANASIA

If you are old enough to love and care for a pony of your own, you are old enough to understand why we must consider this subject: The end of your pony's useful life, whenever that might be.

Ponies, if they have been cared for properly, often live a very long time; I have known several who have lived to be thirty-two years old, and more. (Though, of course, these ponies were not asked to do very much in their last few years.) You may outgrow your pony while he is still young and in good condition, and then selling him or giving him to someone who will love and care for him as you have is the very best thing for both the pony and yourself. Many happy ponies have spent their lives teaching youngsters to ride, going on from family to family as their "pupils" learn and grow. These wise, dear ponies are priceless possessions and are loved and cared for like members of each family.

But should the time come when a pony has grown too old to enjoy his life, or if he should become incurably sick or lame, do not let him go out of your hands for the few dollars you might be able to get for him. Whether you have owned him for just a few months or a number of years makes no difference whatsoever. When he came to you, you accepted the responsibility of his well-being, and it at once became your duty to do whatever was best for his future.

If this means that, in the careful and unhurried opinion of your veterinarian, your pony's useful life should be over, have the courage and kindness to have him gently put to sleep. Though this will be a sad day for you, you will always know that you have done the very best thing for your pony, and that is all that matters.

In a special place in your stable you should keep these first-aid supplies:

A generous jar or tube of healing ointment recommended by your vet.

A bottle of hydrogen peroxide.

A cake of castile soap.

A box of sterile cotton.

A bottle of gentian violet.

Any break in your pony's skin should be treated promptly. Cuts and scrapes should be cleaned with castile soap and warm water, dabbed thoroughly with hydrogen peroxide with a sterile piece of cotton, then covered thickly with healing ointment. Continue using the ointment until the cut has healed.

If, however, your pony develops irritated, moist, or raw patches on his skin which do not show signs of healthy healing within a few days, they may be caused by ringworm, mange, or eczema. These conditions are difficult to diagnose and treat, and you will need the advice of your vet.

Puncture Wounds are deep and narrow. They are caused by such things as pointed twigs or branches, nails, dog bites, or pitchforks. Because puncture wounds close up tightly when the injuring object is pulled out, they seldom bleed enough to get clean and are

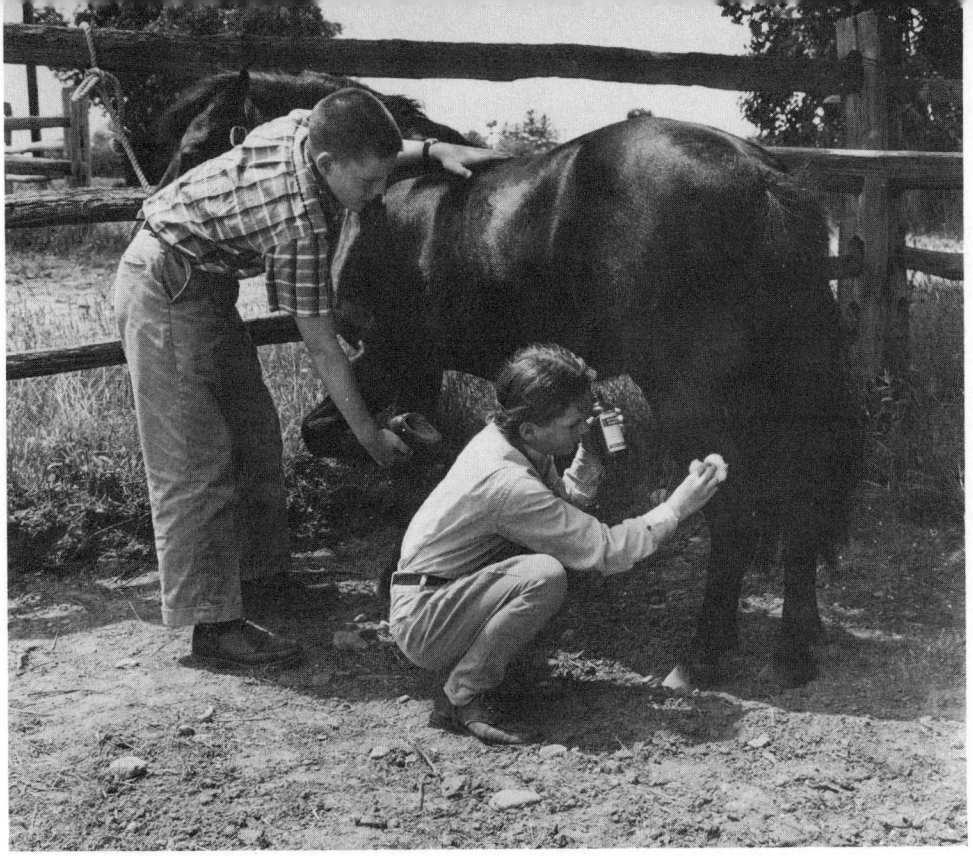

ALL SMALL CUTS AND SCRAPES SHOULD BE TREATED PROMPTLY

hard to treat. They are perfect breeding places for infection.

Puncture wounds need veterinary care.

The germs of tetanus — lockjaw — are always present in and around a stable, which is one reason why all cuts need prompt attention. If the cut is deep enough or of a type to need a vet's care, the vet may give your pony a tetanus shot to prevent infection.

For the same reason, if you are caring for a pony of your own, or if you are around them a great deal, you should tell your own doctor, as he may want you to have preventative tetanus shots. Wear sturdy shoes when you are working in your stable, and NEVER go near a stable barefooted!

Wounds of the Hoof—cuts or punctures in the sole of the hoof or frog—should not be treated by an amateur. It may be necessary to cut part of the hoof away to lessen the danger of infection, and this is a job only a veterinarian can do.

Because of the obvious danger to your pony and to yourself, do be sensible about the care of your stable equipment! Never leave rakes or pitchforks lying on the ground, or in a stall or paddock. Tie your pony up, or shut him outside if you can, while you are using a pitchfork in his stall. Except for medicines which come in bottles, do not use glass containers in your stable and do not let anyone leave empty bottles anywhere near the stable. Nails do not have to be rusty to be dangerous, so make sure there are no boards lying on the ground with nails or screws protruding from them. Protect, cover, or hammer down sharp nails or screws everywhere in your stable.

Rope Burns are real burns; they are not cuts or scrapes! Treat them as burns, using healing ointment on them generously. Rope burns are difficult to cure, since they are generally caused by the pony's getting a leg caught in a tie rope, then struggling to get free. Therefore, these burns are usually on the back of a joint, such as the knee or pastern, so that every step the pony takes for days afterwards breaks the burn open again while you are trying to get it healed.

IT IS BEST TO TIE YOUR PONY UP WHEN YOU ARE USING A PITCHFORK IN HIS STALL

Curing a rope burn is a long and discouraging business which will give you plenty of time to promise yourself not to let this kind of accident happen again, if you can possibly prevent it.

EYE INJURIES. Call your vet if your pony hurts his eye in any way. Do not try to examine it yourself if you find it half-closed, or swollen and weeping. Eye injuries are tricky, and you might increase the damage without meaning to.

BRUISES. Bruises, if they are on soft flesh, seldom need attention. They may cause trouble, however, when they are on a joint or tendon. A bruised joint or tendon will swell, of course, and sometimes if neglected it remains permanently hard and swollen, leaving an unsightly blemish and the possibility of permanent lameness. It is best to have such bruises looked at by a veterinarian, so he can tell you how to treat them properly.

Kicks by other ponies may do no more than cause a light bruise or they may cause quite a lot of damage, depending on the force of the kick and where the blow lands.

Ponies turned out together in a paddock or pasture may be a pretty sight, but ponies are like people; some of them get along well with each other and some do not. Turning two ponies out together can be a bit of a risk, especially if they are wearing shoes, which increase the damage done by kicking.

Turning two strange ponies out together often causes trouble. Let the two ponies get to know each other for a few days, then watch them carefully when they first go out together. If you can, have their hind shoes taken off. Separate them immediately if they start to scuffle and fight.

There is little you can do with a scrappy pony except to keep him by himself.

Never feed two ponies grain when they are within kicking distance of each other. Even a mild-tempered pony will kick his companion if he thinks he might try to steal his grain.

Saddle Sores are caused by the rubbing and chafing of tack against a pony's skin. Be sure to keep all your tack clean and soft and make sure the pony's coat is well brushed where the saddle, girth, and bridle go, before you start out for a ride. Saddle sores take a long time to heal; it is much easier to prevent them than it is to cure them.

The soft skin just behind a pony's elbow is a spot often neglected in grooming and one of the first places girth sores start, helped along by unbrushed mud or sweat.

At the first sign of a saddle sore, touch the spot with gentian violet. If the sore is bad enough to be open and raw, alternate gentian violet one day and healing ointment the next. The tack that caused the trouble must not go back on your pony until the sore is completely healed.

Ponies who have not been worked for some time are more prone to saddle sores, since their skin has become soft. It helps to sponge the saddle and girth area of such ponies with a solution of table salt in warm water, once a day, for a week or ten days. This helps toughen the skin and makes it less prone to chafing.

Scratches, or Cracked Heels, are names for an irritation that appears on a pony's heels or on the backs of his pasterns. If left untreated, the irritation can turn into flaming sores which can make your pony lame.

Scratches are caused by dampness, such as keeping a pony in a wet stall or muddy paddock, or by forgetting to brush his heels and the backs of his pasterns thoroughly during grooming, because dust and sweat run down his legs and collect in the soft, tender hollows of his heels. A moment spent drying these spots with a towel after your pony has been sponged off, or has been out in the rain or mud, helps prevent this problem.

Though scratches do not lame your pony permanently, they cause a great deal of swelling and soreness while they last and, like rope burns, they tend to crack open as the pony moves. Healing ointment applied several times a day helps to keep the cracking to a minimum while the sores heal.

Severe Bleeding is more or less unusual in ponies, because the major veins and arteries are well protected. But if your pony should receive such a deep wound that he starts to bleed a great deal, hold or bandage a clean white cloth firmly against the wound until the vet arrives. This cloth may be anything white and clean, from a bath towel to a handful of handkerchiefs. The cloth need not be sterile.

Do not waste time fussing with anything you might have heard about tourniquets. They usually do far more harm than good.

Patent Medicines—remedies that can be bought in a store—are to be avoided, whether they are for worms, coughs, or any pony illnesses. If your pony is sick enough to need medicine, he is sick enough to need a vet to choose the proper medicine for him and to tell you what to do.

POISONS. Many insect and weed sprays are poisons. Do not let your pony snatch mouthfuls of grass as you ride and make sure he cannot get into an orchard where trees have been sprayed. Be careful with sprays you may use in the stable; make sure the label says the spray is harmless to animals and, even then, keep it from falling on your pony's grain or hay.

Do not put any spray directly on your pony without advice from your vet.

Use mousetraps in the stable instead of poison.

The leaves of some weeds, shrubs, and trees become poisonous after they have been cut and have begun to wilt. Wild cherry is one example, and there are several others. Clean up all cut weeds or fallen branches your pony can reach in his paddock or pasture.

The symptoms of poisoning are very like those of colic. When you call the vet, be sure to tell him if you suspect your pony may have been eating anything which might have been sprayed with a weed killer or insect poison, so he can bring the necessary antidotes with him.

Selection and Care of Tack

Saddles and bridles are called "tack"; when you put the saddle and bridle on your pony, you are said to "tack him up."

Good tack is cheap insurance against accidents. Make sure all the equipment you have for your pony is of good quality, strong, well-made, and in excellent condition.

Tack may be bought new or secondhand. If it is new, go over every bit of leather with a good leather conditioner before you use it for the first time. This prevents dust and sweat from working into the leather before it is protected.

Plain neat's-foot oil is often used as a conditioner, but it oozes out of the leather for some time, staining the rider's clothes and the pony's coat and making the leather slippery. It also has the tendency to rot stitching. For these reasons the conditioners sold under trade names, which do not have these faults, are better than neat's-foot oil.

Since the different bits and bridles, their adjustment, and the proper fitting of bits, are discussed thoroughly in my other book, *Horsemanship for Beginners,* it would seem unnecessary to repeat it all again. However, here are a few important reminders:

The saddle must not press on your pony's withers. Check this while you are sitting in the saddle. You should be able to slip all the fingers of one hand between the pommel (the front of the saddle) and your pony's withers. If you cannot do this, you must use a pad of some kind to protect the withers.

Make sure the saddle does not press anywhere on your pony's spine.

The bridle must lie smooth and untwisted on your pony's head. The bit must be just wide enough to fit your pony's mouth without pinching, but must not be so wide that it slides back and forth in his mouth as you put pressure on the reins. Adjust the cheek straps so the bit hangs evenly and fits snugly in the corners of the mouth without wrinkling the lips.

The reins must not be so long that they hang in a loop near your foot as you ride. A shoe repair shop can shorten them if they are too long.

The bar which holds the stirrup leather on an English saddle must have a safety catch and this catch should always be left down.

The stirrup iron should be about an inch and a half wider than the ball of your shoe or boot. You will have to get larger stirrup irons as you grow.

The stirrups on a Western saddle must be the right size for your foot; if the stirrup is too small, your shoe might jam into it too tightly; if it is too big, your foot might slip all the way through and get caught.

(And, though this has nothing to do with tack, *never* ride in sneakers because they have no heel to prevent your foot from slipping through the stirrup.)

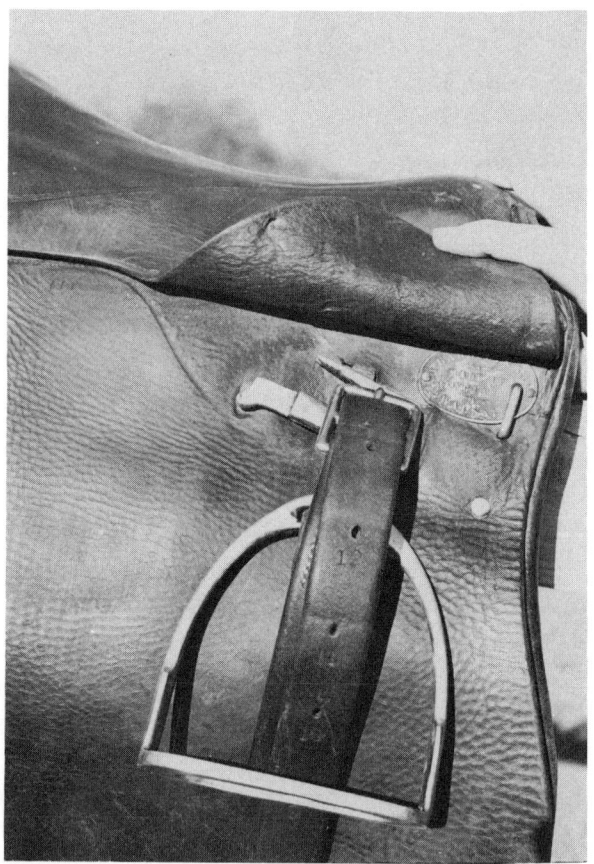

SAFETY CATCH FOR STIRRUP
(LEAVE IN OPEN POSITION)

CORRECT WIDTH OF STIRRUP

CARE OF TACK

After each use, clean the worst of the mud and dust off your tack with a dampened sponge. Rinse the sponge, rub it lightly over a cake of saddle soap, and work the soap well into the leather.

Be particularly fussy about keeping the under side of your saddle, and all of your girth, soft and clean.

Once every month or six weeks, take all your tack apart. Dampen your sponge with leather conditioner instead of water, use a little saddle soap, and go over every inch of leather, paying particular attention to the spots where the leather bends, such as the reins at the bit and the stirrup leather where the iron rests.

Use any good metal polish on bits and buckles. Be sure to rinse the bit well.

If your tack should get a soaking in a rainstorm, let it dry away from artificial heat of any kind, then go over it with leather conditioner. Rain will not hurt tack that has been well cared for.

Do not forget that your halter is made of leather too, and gets even tougher use than your bridle and saddle. Give it a good conditioning and cleaning every now and then.

You and Your Pony

As this book was being written, my ponies from the past seemed to haunt every page. There was Mokey, whose dear brown and white face kept coming back because she was my first pony, and taught me the most. There was Monte Carlo, who was gray and beautiful and not very good at anything he did, and who jumped out of his paddock one autumn afternoon and ate rotten apples for two hours in the neighbor's orchard. (He had the worst case of colic I have ever seen.)

There was Rosie, all of eight-and-a-half hands high, who climbed stone walls like a little goat, and Red Robin, Mokey's foal, who played tag with our beagle in the snow and who liked to go swimming all by himself in the pasture pond. . . .

Ponies are people. Each is an individual, with special likes and dislikes of his own. The owner who never goes near his pony except to ride can never be sure what his pony is really like, because he does not take care of him. It is in the daily working with a pony, feeding and grooming and handling him, that the owner has the chance to *know* his pony, and the rewards and satisfaction of ownership are increased this way more than words can tell.

You are facing a tremendous responsibility when you accept the care of a pony, for his life and future are in your hands. But this in itself is a wonderful thing, for it means that your pony's bright eyes, glowing coat, and his over-all look of well-being are the results of *your* efforts, *your* knowledge, and *your* care.

This cannot help but add to the enjoyment of your pony in everything you do together. And there are so many things to do! There are branches of the United States Pony Club all over the country, with more being added every year. The Pony Club can be joined by anyone under the age of twenty-one, riders of horses as well as ponies. The Club offers the companionship of other riders at meetings and rallies, and good teaching by qualified instructors on horsemanship and stable care. (If you would like to know more about the Pony Club, and the name of the branch nearest you, write to Mrs. John A. Reidy, Secretary, United States Pony Club; Pleasant Street, Dover, Massachusetts.)

There are merit badges to be earned by Boy and Girl Scouts; pony shows and gymkhanas to enter; picnic rides and cross-country rides with friends; fox hunting in many parts of the country—the list is endless. And, above all these activities with your pony, there is the fun of riding just for its own sake.

And may you discover, as you ride your pony and work with him, the pleasure and the challenge in learning to care for a pony of your own.

Glossary

Age: January first is considered the birthday of all ponies, regardless of the months in which they were born. (Even though a pony may have been born in March or April, for instance, the following January first will be his first birthday.)

Age Terminology:

Foal: A pony from the day of his or her birth until he or she is weaned (usually between four and six months of age).

Weanling: A pony who has been weaned but who is not yet a year old.

Yearling: A pony between one and two years of age.

Two-Year-Old, Three-Year-Old, etc. Terms used to describe ages of ponies.

Aged: Term used to cover all ages over nine years.

Crossbred: A pony of mixed breeding. This term is usually used to describe a pony with one parent of known pure breeding, and the other parent of another pure breed, or of mixed breeding. For example: A pony with a purebred Welsh sire and a purebred Shetland dam would be a crossbred pony. (Such a pony can also be called a "Welsh-Shetland cross.")

Dam: The mother of a pony.

Euthanasia: Putting a pony (or any other animal) painlessly to sleep so he never wakes up again. This is a kind and thoughtful thing to do when a pony is too old to enjoy his life, or when he is suffering from an incurable and painful illness or lameness.

Float: To smooth the rough and jagged edges of a pony's teeth with a special rasp. (This rasp is also called a "float.")

Hand: Ponies and horses are measured in **hands.** One hand equals four inches. If a pony is fifty-four inches high he is thirteen hands, two inches high, thirteen and a half hands, or thirteen-two; this can be written in numbers—13.2.

A pony's height is determined by measuring him from the ground to the top of his **withers** (the highest part of his shoulder; see diagram, page 111).

Fifty-eight inches (fourteen and a half hands, or 14.2) is the dividing line of height between ponies and horses. A pony may be any height up to and including 14.2. A horse may be any height over 14.2.

Near Side: The left side of a pony (when you and the pony are facing the same direction).

Off Side: The right side of a pony (when you and the pony are facing the same direction). In horsemen's terminology, it is correct to use the words "near" and "off" instead of "left" and "right" when referring to a part of a pony. For example, you would say, "My pony is lame in the **near** foreleg" instead of calling it the "left foreleg." Or, "My pony has a grass stain on his **off** shoulder" instead of "right shoulder."

Paddock: A small, enclosed, fenced area near or adjoining a stable.

Pasture: A large fenced area, usually with grass suitable for grazing.

Purebred: A pony of pure breeding; one of a long line of ponies of a specific pure breed (such as the Welsh Ponies, Shetland Ponies, Connemara Ponies, etc.) The word **purebred** is sometimes confused with **thoroughbred;** in horsemen's terminology, the word **Thoroughbred** (capitalized) is generally used only in reference to the Thoroughbred breed of horse.

Sex Terminology:

Filly: A young **female** pony (up to and including four years of age).

Colt: A young **male** pony (up to and including four years of age). These two words **filly** and **colt** are used to indicate the sex of a young pony, in combination with the age terminology explained at the beginning of this glossary. For example, it is correct to say **filly foal** or **colt foal;** weanling filly (or colt); yearling, two-, three-, or four-year-old filly (or colt).

Mare: A female pony over the age of four years.

Stallion: An unaltered male pony over the age of four years.

Gelding: A male pony which has been physically altered to make him more gentle and more easily managed.

Sire: The father of a pony.

Sound: A **sound** pony is healthy, with normal eyesight, wind, and heart. He is not lame, and he is free from scars or blemishes which, in the opinion of the examining veterinarian, might one day interfere with the pony's usefulness.

Staring: Term used to describe a pony's coat when it is dry and harsh, looking as though it were standing on end; a sign of illness.

Vetting: The examination of a pony, by a qualified veterinarian, to determine the pony's health and soundness.

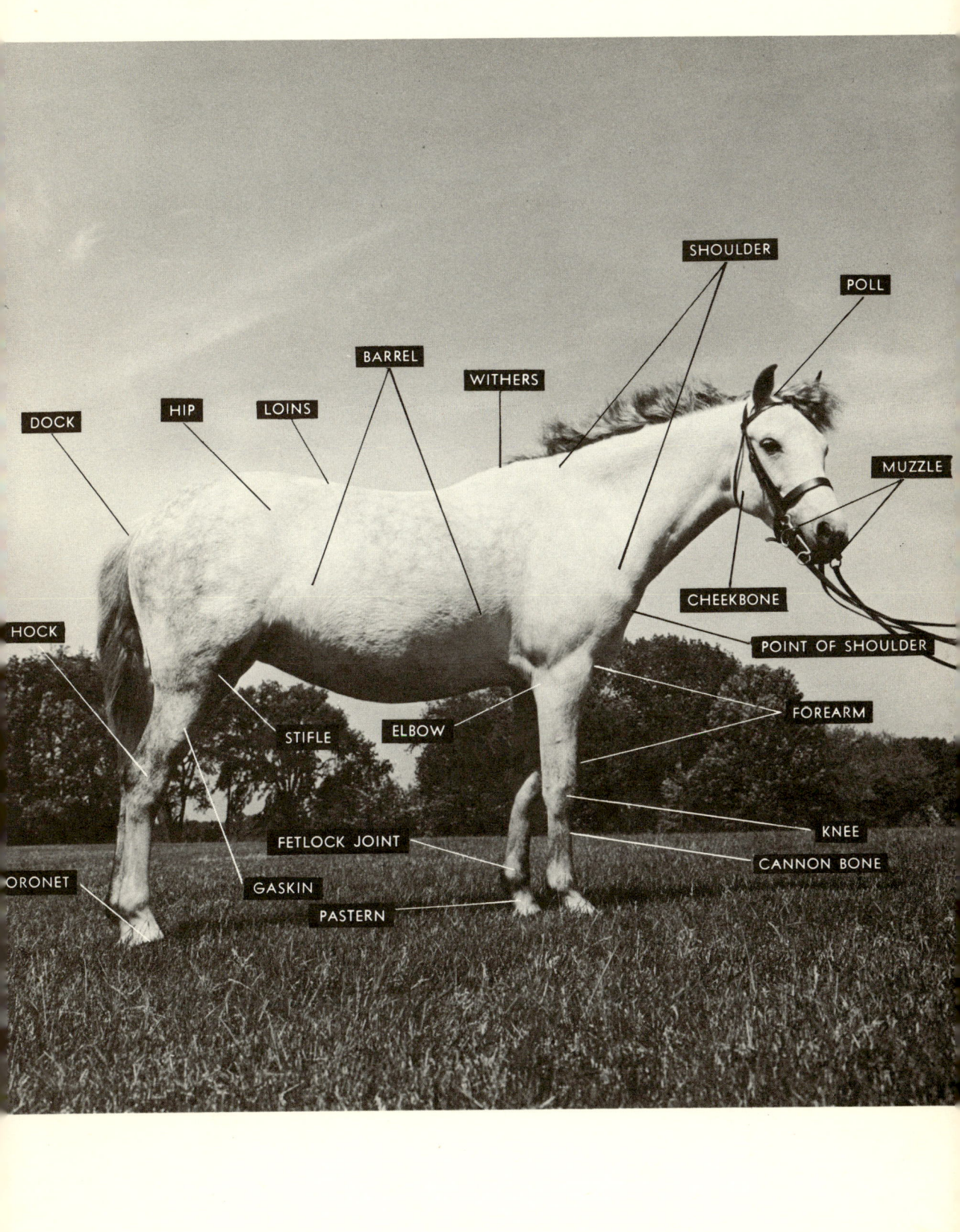

Index

accidents: cuts, 100; eye injuries, 99; with fences, 37, 39; getting "cast," 25–6; getting caught, 17, 25, 31, 38, 49, 68, 71, 98; kicks, 99; poisons, 101; riding, 84; rope burns, 19, 25, 98–9, 100; saddle sores, 99–100; in stable, 33, 34, 36, 46, 50, 98; *and see* tangling
age of pony, 4, 13–4, 109–10
alfalfa, 49
appetite, loss of, 89
apples, 92, 107
azoturia, 84–6
balance, 7, 10, 77, 78, 86
bandage, 100–1
barefooted, going, 97
barrel, 9; illustrated, 111
bathing, 64, 75
bedding, 33, 41–2, 57; care of, 42–3; eating of, 41, 49; storage of, 34
birthdays, 109
biting, 28, 29, 55
bits, 19, 22, 103, 105
blacksmith, 77–81
blankets, 63, 68–71; care of, 71–2
bleeding, 100–1
blueing, 62–3, 64
body brush, 60–1
boots, 104
Boy Scouts, 108
braiding, 65
bran, 52–4, 92
breaking, 4, 13; loose, 22
breeding, 4–5; mixed, 109; pure, 109–10
bridle, 12, 19, 20, 22, 23, 25, 36, 63, 100, 103; breaking of, 22; leading with, 19
bruises, 33, 59, 79, 81, 84, 99
brushes, 59–62, 64, 81
brushing, 59–63, 99–100; of sheets and blankets, 71–2; position of hands in, 59–61
buckets, 45–6, 54, 58
bucking, 55, 68
burlap, 54
burns, rope, 19, 25, 98–9, 100
burrs, 62
buying a pony, 3–15; qualities to look for in, 6–11
calking, 79–80
cannon bone, illustrated, 111
cantering, 12, 87
carelessness, 28, 36, 81
carrots, 54

cart, two-wheeled, 42
"cast," 25–6
catching, 22–3, 29
ceilings, for stall, 31–3
chasing, 23, 28, 29
cheek straps, 103
cheekbone, illustrated, 111
chest, 10; straps, 70–1
children: ponies for, 14–15; teaching to ride, 95
chilling, 64, 68, 94
choosing a pony, 3–15
climbing, 38, 107
clinches, 79
clipping, 67–9; machines, 64, 68–9
clothes for riding, 103
clover, 49
club meetings, 108
coat: appearance of, 88–9, 91, 107, 110; care of, 57, 62–4, 67–9, 71, 75, 99, 103; spring and winter, 67
cold weather care, 41, 67–8
colds, 91, 101
colic, 26, 48, 55, 85, 91–3, 94, 101, 107; flatulent, 92; spasmodic, 85, 92
colt, 110
confinement, 26, 36
conformation, 7–11
Connemara Ponies, 110
corn, 52, 92
coronet, illustrated, 111
cost of pony, 4–5
cotton, sterile, 96
coughs, *see* colds
"cow hocks," 10
cracked heels, 100
cribbing, or crib biting, 26, 27; strap, 27
crippling, 75
crop, riding, 29
crossbred pony, 11, 109
crowding, 28–9
currycombs, 58–9, 60–1, 67
currying, 57, 59
cuts, 100–101
daily care, 3, 57, 63, 81, 107
dam, 109
dampness, 43, 100
dandy brush, 59–60, 61, 62, 72
dangerous ponies, 29
discipline, 17–21, 23–5, 28–9
dismounting, 12

disposition, 12
dock, 61, 62; illustrated, 111
dogs, 36, 96, 107
doors, for stall, 33–4; Dutch, 33–4, 72
doorways: height of, 31, 33; leading through, 24
drainage, for stall, 33
drugs, see *medicine*
dry-quart measure, 51
ears, 8, 20, 59, 61, 75, 89
eczema, 96
elbow, illustrated, 111
euthanasia, 95–6, 109
exercise, 36, 51, 57, 67–8; lack of, 26, 84, 94
experts, advice from, 11, 29
expression, 88, 89, 91, 92
eyes: injuries, 99; sight, 13; width between, 8
face, 15, 46
falling down, 84
feeding, 19, 28, 47–55, 57, 84–5, 88, 94, 107; care in, 91–2; changes in, 55, 92; cost of, 55; quality of, 90–1; quantity of, 49–55, 84–5, 94; two ponies, 99
female, 110
fences, 36–9, 110; injuries from, 36–7, 39
fetlock, 10, 80, 83; illustrated, 111
fever, 89, 94
fighting, 99
filly, 110
first aid, 80, 96–101; supplies, 36, 96
flies, 72
floating, 90, 109
flooring, for stall, 33
foal, 109–10
forearm, illustrated, 111
forelegs, 10, 61; lameness in, 83
forelock: cleaning, 62; leading by, 20; trimming, 64
forging, 78
founder, 85, 93–4
fox hunting, 108
freedom, 23, 36
fright, 17, 22, 28, 29, 33, 37, 49
frog, 77, 79, 81
frost nails, *see* sharpshoeing
galloping, 87
garages, 31
garbage cans, 34
gaskin, illustrated, 111
gates, 38–9; leading through, 23, 24
gelding, 110
gentian violet, 96, 100
Girl Scouts, 108
girth, 63, 75, 86, 100, 105; sores, *see* saddle sores
glass, danger from, 34, 98

"goose rump," 10
grain, 41, 48, 51–2, 54, 55, 84, 85, 92, 94, 99, 101; purchase, 52; stealing, 99; storage, 34
grass, 47–50, 51, 52, 55, 101, 110
grazing, 19, 48, 110
greediness, 23, 41
grooming, 28, 57–65, 68, 88, 100, 107; equipment, 34, 57; for show, 62
gymkhanas, 108
habits: bad, 5, 14; learning through imitation, 26; nervous, 26–7; *and see* vices
halter, 3, 11, 17–20, 22, 24, 36, 57, 105; fit of, 17, 19; leading with, 19
handling, 3, 12, 17, 19–29, 107; improper, 23, 24, 28
hands, measurement by, 109
hard surfaces, 93; *and see* roads
hay, 41, 48–51, 55, 92, 101; buying of, 49; storage of, 34, 49
"hay belly," 41
head, 8, 9, 19, 25, 75, 103; accidents to, 33, 34
health, bad, signs of, 88–9
heatstroke, 73
heaves, 91, 94
heels, 61, 100
height, 109
help, getting, 25–6, 84, 86
hidebound, 89
hindquarters, 10; bruising, 24
hip, illustrated, 111
hocks, 10, 75; illustrated, 111
holding, 24
hoof: beat, 82; dressing, 80; pick, 81
hoofs, 10, 61, 77–8; care of, 62, 63, 77–82; damage to, 94; picking up, 80–1; swelling of, 93; wounds of, 97
hooks, 36, 46
Horsemanship for Beginners, 103
horses, 107, 109, 110
hose, for bathing, 64, 75
hot weather care, 67, 72–3, 75
hunters, 5, 11
hydrogen peroxide, 96
idleness, 26, 27
illness, 84–6, 88–96, 101, 110; incurable, 96, 109; prevention of, 95
infection, 97
insulation, 33
intelligence, 8
jaws, 19, 20, 61, 75
jogging, 82
joint: bruises on, 99; fetlock, 10
jumping, 36, 38, 87, 107; jumpers, 5
kicking, 23, 28, 29, 55; by other ponies, 99
knees, 10, 75; illustrated, 111
lameness, 13, 24, 77, 79, 81–4, 96, 99, 100, 110; detecting, 81–4; incurable, 96, 99, 109; sudden, 84

[113]

lamina, 77
laxatives, 52, 53
lead ropes, 19–20, 22–5, 36, 48
leading, 20–1, 23, 24–5
leather conditioner, 103, 105
leaves, poisonous, 101
legs, 10, 75, 77; breaking of, 49; care of, 86–7; hind, 61, 75; movement of, 81; *and see* accidents; getting caught *and* tangling
light bulbs, 34
light-colored ponies, 62, 64
life, length of, 95; *and see* euthanasia
lime, 43
linseed meal, 52
lockjaw, *see* tetanus
loins, illustrated, 111
loose box, *see* stall, box
lying down, 43, 70, 89, 92; in stall, 25
male, 110
mane: care of, 62–5; combs, 62
mange, 96
mangers, iron, 50, 54
manners, 6–7, 24–5
manure, 43, 72, 91
mashes, hot, 53–4
meanness, 5, 15, 28–9
measurement, 51; *and see* hands
medicines, 86, 98; patent, 101
merit badges, 108
metal polish, 105
mice, 34
misbehavior, *see* manners
mischief, 15, 17, 28
molasses, 52
"Monday morning disease," 84
moth balls, 72
mounting, 12
mousetraps, 101
mouth, hurting of, 22
mow burning, 49
muzzle, 8, 19, 20, 28, 46; care of, 75; illustrated, 111
nails, 39, 96, 98, 99
near side, 109
neat's-foot oil, 103
neck, 8, 9; rubbing, 65; tying by, 22
nervous habits, *see* habits
newspaper advertisements, 4
nipping, playful, 28
nodding, 82
nose band, 19
oat: measure, 23; straw, 41
oats, 23, 52, 53-4; whole, 52
obedience, 12, 23, 29; *and see* discipline
off side, 109
ointment, 96, 98, 100
old age, 109; *and see* euthanasia
outgrowing pony, 95
overeating, 92, 107

overfeeding, 84, 94
ownership of pony, 4, 95, 107–8
pad, 103
paddock, 17, 23, 27, 29, 34, 36, 45, 67, 68, 81, 92, 98, 99, 100, 101, 107, 110; cleaning of, 43; fences for, 36–8; gates for, 38–9; shade in, 73; size of, 36
panicking, *see* fright
pasterns, 10, 61, 100; illustrated, 111
pasture, 23, 27, 29, 48, 57, 67, 72, 81, 101, 107, 110; water supply in, 47
pasturing, 55; summer, 72–3; two ponies together, 99; winter, 67
peat moss, 41–2
pitchforks, 36, 43, 96, 98
pointing, 83
points of pony, 8; illustrated, 111
poisons, 101
poll, illustrated, 111
pommel, 103
post-and-rail fencing, 36, 38
prices of ponies, *see* cost
purchase of pony, *see* buying
purebred, 110
rats, 34
reins, 20, 22, 86, 103, 105; in leading, 19; length of, 104
rest, 84–5
rewards, 23
riding, 12, 63, 67, 75, 77, 79, 81, 82, 84–5, 87, 91, 94, 101, 104, 107–8; cross-country, 108; instruction, 3, 108; overdoing, 93; picnic, 108; summer, 73; *and see* roads
riding stable, 68, 78
ring, 12
ringworm, 96
roads, 12, 78, 87; *and see* hard surfaces
rolling, 26, 68, 92
rope, 49; *and see* burns, rope
rope hay nets, 50
rubber bands, 65
rump, 10; *and see* "goose rump"
runaway, *see* catching
saddle, 9, 12, 63, 75, 86, 99, 103, 105; English, 104; fit of, 103; Western, 104
saddle soap, 105
saddle sores, 99–100
salt: brick, 54; iodized, 54; table, 46, 54, 100
scars, 110
schooling, 4, 13
scratches, 100
screens, 34, 72
selling, 95–6
shade, 73
sharpshoeing, 79–80
shedding, 67
sheds, 31

[114]

sheets, 70–1; care of, 71–2
sheep hurdle fencing, 36–7
Shetland Ponies, 9–10, 51, 109, 110
shoeing, 83
shoes, 77–9; damage from, 99; loss of, 79; *and see* sharpshoeing
shoulder, 8–9, 10, 19; illustrated, 111; point of, illustrated, 111
shows, 4, 108; grooming for, 62; show ponies, 4–5, 11
sire, 110
skin, 100; breaks in, 96; *and see* coat
sleeping, 43
small ponies, 15, 67
snarls, 62
sneakers, 104
snow, 87, 107
soap, 62, 64; castile, 96; *and see* saddle
soundness, 82, 110
spine, 103
sponges, 61, 105
sponging, 64, 75, 81, 94, 100
sprays, 101
stable, 31, 33, 34, 36, 97, 110; equipment, 36, 98; *and see* riding stable *and* stall
staggering, 84
stains, 62
stall, 11–12, 17, 25–7, 28–9, 31, 34, 45, 46, 50, 67, 70, 85, 92, 94, 98, 100; box, 31; building of, 31, 33; care of, 41–3, 81; size of, 31; standing or straight, 31
stall walking, 26–7
stallion, 110
staking out, 49
staring, 110
stiffness, 85
stifle, illustrated, 111
stirrups, 12, 20, 104–5
stomach, 41, 91; *and see* colic
stones, getting out, 84
stone walls, 38, 107
storage room, 34
straw, 41
striking, 29
stubbornness, 17, 24, 81
stumbling, 78–9, 83
sugar cane, 42
suitability, 6–7, 29
sunstroke, 73
surcingles, 69, 70, 71
sweat scraper, 75
sweating, 85, 92, 94
sweet feeds, 52

swimming, 107
swollen glands, 91
tack, 100; care of, 99, 105; fitting of, 103–4; purchase of, 103; to tack up, 103; *and see* saddle sores
tail: care of, 62–3; rubbing, 91
tangling, 17, 25, 31, 38, 49, 68, 71, 98; *and see* accidents; getting caught
teasing, 28, 29
teeth: care of, 89–91, 109
tendons, 99
tetanus, 97
Thoroughbred, 110
throat, 8, 61
thrush, 43, 81
tie ropes, 22, 31
timothy, 49
tourniquets, 101
trimming, 64
trotting, 12, 82, 87
turning: in circle, 17; loose, 23
unbroken colt, 4
United States Pony Club, 107–8
veterinarian, 13, 52, 54, 78, 79, 84, 90, 91, 92, 94–5, 96, 97, 101; examination by, 13, 91, 110; fees of, 95; when to call, 86, 94, 99, 101
vices, 28–9
vomiting, 91
walking, 12, 87, 94
warming up, 87
washing, *see* bathing
water: cold, 64, 75, 94; salt, 81
watering, 45–7, 57, 92, 94
weanling, 109
weaving, 26–7
weed killers, 101
weediness, 9
Welsh: Ponies, 109, 110; Shetland cross, 109
wheat straw, 41
wild ponies, 17
wind sucking, 26–7
windows, for stall, 34
winter, *see* cold weather
wire: barbed, 37–8; fencing, 37
withers, 8, 103, 109; illustrated, 111
wood shavings, 42
working, 47, 51, 68, 77, 93, 100, 107–8
worms, 90–1, 101
wounds: deep, 100–1; of hoof, 97; puncture, 96–7
yearling, 109–10

ABOUT THE AUTHOR

Jean Slaughter has been active in the horse show world for a number of years, first in riding her own ponies and horses as well as exhibiting, as an amateur, for other owners. She is an American Horse Shows Association Recognized Judge in Hunters, Jumpers, and Hunter Seat Equitation, and has judged the Hunter Ponies division and Hunter Seat Equitation at the National Horse Show in Madison Square Garden.

She has hunted in England and in Ireland where she was, for several years, a member of the South County Dublin Harriers.

Miss Slaughter now lives in North Stamford, Connecticut with her artist-husband, Roy Doty, and her son, Christopher.

Text set in LINOTYPE TIMES ROMAN. *Composed by* H. O. BULLARD, INC., NEW YORK.
Printed by THE MURRAY PRINTING COMPANY, FORGE VILLAGE, MASSACHUSETTS.
Bound by H. WOLFF, NEW YORK.
Paper manufactured by P. H. GLATFELTER COMPANY, SPRING GROVE, PENNSYLVANIA.